BEYOND DISCIPLINARITY

This book provides a means of comprehensively grounding and considering the epistemological and philosophical underpinnings of practice-based research epistemologies. By introducing readers to the diverse array of methodological tools and concepts that are necessary to underpin postgraduate research, this book develops an understanding of the distinctions between practice-led research, practice-based research and question-led research, and the contextual significance of each, as well as enabling students to comprehend the historical relationships between academic disciplines and the value of reconnecting them at an epistemological and philosophical level. Through illustrated examples from applied practice across disciplines such as art, social sciences and medical and allied healthcare sciences, readers are encouraged to develop the capacity to not only think conceptually about their own research, but to systematically evaluate that of others. With this focus on descriptive studies from practice, the book fosters higher-order critical thinking in relation to implications for methodological implementation, encouraging deep learning processes and the confidence to transcend the limits of one's own discipline in order to work collaboratively with researchers in different fields.

Catherine Hayes is Professor of Health Professions Pedagogy and Scholarship in the Faculty of Applied Sciences at the University of Sunderland, UK. She is also a National Teaching Fellow, Principal Fellow of the Higher Education Academy and Visiting Professor in Higher Education at the Universities of Cumbria and Liverpool Hope. Catherine is Secretary of the International Federation of National Teaching Fellows and works with the Ministry of Defence's Medical Defence Academy in framing military epistemology within a modernised education and training curriculum for tripartite services provision.

John Fulton is Director of Postgraduate Research and Associate Professor of Research-Based Practice at the University of Sunderland and co-editor of *Studying Postgraduate Healthcare: A Pre-Reader, The Professional Doctorate* and *Mentorship in Healthcare*.

Andrew Livingstone is Professor of Ceramics at the National Glass Centre, University of Sunderland, where he leads CARCuos (Ceramic Arts Research Centre) and is supervisor to PhD researchers. Andrew has authored and contributed to numerous books including *The Ceramics Reader*. As an artist and researcher, his exhibitions include the Smithsonian Institute and the Garth Clark Gallery, New York. His work is held in many private and public collections internationally, including Yingge Ceramics Museum, Taiwan, and the Garth Clark and Mark Del Vecchio Permanent Collection at the Museum of Fine Arts, Houston. He is a Senior Fellow of the Higher Education Academy and a member of the International Academy of Ceramics.

Claire Todd is an artist who works in sculpture, performance and installation, exhibiting works locally and internationally, including public sculpture in the Netherlands and Belgium. She studied Sculpture at Northumbria University and MA Scenography at St Martin's, London. Subsequent to that, she attended the postgraduate programme in sculpture at the Rijksakademie, Amsterdam. In 2003–2004, Claire was recipient of the Helen Chadwick Fellowship to the British School at Rome and Oxford University and, in 2008, she received an NEA award to Corpus Christi University, Texas. Alongside this, Claire is a successful and much respected AHRC PhD graduate in the Department of Ceramics and Glass at the University of Sunderland.

Stephen Capper is a professional doctorate student in the Faculty of Health Sciences and Wellbeing at the University of Sunderland. A podiatrist and academic by professional background, Stephen's work has explored the notion of epistemology as applied to clinical sciences, specifically biomechanics. His groundbreaking work is among the first to ever challenge the basis of scientific knowledge in podiatric medicine in relation to the claim of evidence-based praxis across this clinical discipline.

Peter Smith is Emeritus Professor of Computing. He joined the University of Sunderland as an undergraduate student in 1975 and received his doctorate in 1981. Since then, he has held several teaching, research and management positions at the university, including Dean and Chair of the University Research Degrees Committee. He has published over 250 papers, and has supervised and examined over 100 doctoral candidates at universities in the UK, Europe and Hong Kong. Peter is a Fellow of the British Computer Society and Principal Fellow of the Higher Education Academy. He has published extensively on a range of subjects including computing, management and doctoral studies, particularly in relation to professional doctorates.

Routledge Advances in Research Methods

For more information about this series, please visit: www.routledge.com/
Routledge-Advances-in-Research-Methods/book-series/RARM

BEYOND DISCIPLINARITY

Historical Evolutions of Research Epistemology

Catherine Hayes, John Fulton and Andrew Livingstone with Claire Todd, Stephen Capper and Peter Smith

LONDON AND NEW YORK

First published 2021
by Routledge
2 Park Square, Milton Park, Abingdon, Oxon OX14 4RN

and by Routledge
52 Vanderbilt Avenue, New York, NY 10017

Routledge is an imprint of the Taylor & Francis Group, an informa business

British Library Cataloguing-in-Publication Data
A catalogue record for this book is available from the British Library

Library of Congress Cataloging-in-Publication Data
Names: Hayes, Catherine, author.
Title: Beyond disciplinarity : historical evolutions of research
epistemology / Catherine Hayes [and five others].
Description: Milton Park, Abingdon, Oxon; New York, NY: Routledge, 2021. |
Includes bibliographical references and index.
Identifiers: LCCN 2020031065 (print) | LCCN 2020031066 (ebook) |
ISBN 9781138090934 (paperback) | ISBN 9781138090927 (hardback) |
ISBN 9781315108377 (ebook)
Subjects: LCSH: Social sciences–Research. | Knowledge, Theory of.
Classification: LCC H62 .H345 2021 (print) |
LCC H62 (ebook) | DDC 300.72–dc23
LC record available at https://lccn.loc.gov/2020031065
LC ebook record available at https://lccn.loc.gov/2020031066

ISBN: 9781138090927 (hbk)
ISBN: 9781138090934 (pbk)
ISBN: 9781315108377 (ebk)

Typeset in Bembo
by Newgen Publishing UK

CONTENTS

ACKNOWLEDGEMENTS

Teaching epistemology is more rewarding than challenging in an inter-disciplinary doctoral context, but what is evident is that the fundamental differences in signature pedagogies and intellectual academic disciplines actually transect at given points of historical progression. This book aims to illuminate the reconnections of epistemology at a philosophical level, so that doctoral students, in particular, might consider widening their scope of intellectual thought and reconnecting the epistemological basis of their studies at a far more authentic level that they (or we) first recognised might be possible.

The impetus for writing this book originated from two sources. First, the work we have undertaken within and between our native faculty of Applied Sciences, and the remaining four faculties of Business and Law, Creative Industries, Education and Society and Computing, Engineering and Technology, has actively enabled us to transcend disciplinarity in our own professional practice. We thank all staff of these faculties for their willingness to share an insight into these fields of practice. Second, we have been truly privileged to work as doctoral supervisors across a vast array of interdisciplinary studies and are humbled by the consequent impact of this research by our doctoral candidates in practice. For this we thank, most importantly, those amazing doctoral students, too numerous to mention, who continue to inspire, motivate and energise our own contribution to these programmes and our roles as academics.

We would like to thank all at Routledge, for their unfailing belief in our potential contribution to knowledge from the initial proposal through to its completion.

This book is dedicated in its entirety to Dr Helen Mary Pepper, who never seeks to intellectualise the real truth of this world and who inspires us with the only wisdom that matters.

Professor Catherine Hayes
June 2020

INTRODUCTION

Catherine Hayes

As editors of this text we would like to provide a contextual backdrop as to why the original idea for this book came into existence. Like many higher education institutions, ours has afforded us valuable opportunities to teach on a range of interdisciplinary programmes, where the nature of knowledge is often contested, positioned and debated in abstraction from holistic perspectives surrounding where it might potentially have greatest influence. Nowhere is this truer than in our engagement with postgraduate students, for whom epistemology is not only a new addition to their academic lexicon; it can also provide an opportunity to venture into centuries of philosophical literature. How the real-life application of epistemology in 21st-century professional practice can be applied, as a consequence of this, is often more challenging and less accessible than it ought or ever needs to be. As educators, we became acutely and collectively aware that, in sourcing texts for our students, few books actually provide a means of comprehensively grounding and considering the epistemological and philosophical underpinnings of approaches to research that incorporate a historical perspective, but which also permit their contemporaneous understanding. Without this, the temptation for students to build confidence in adding to new epistemological approaches can potentially be stunted; and this is particularly true in our encouragement of students to transcend disciplinarity in their address of both question-led research and creative artistic praxis.

By introducing the diverse array of methodological tools and concepts that are necessary to underpin postgraduate research, this book develops an understanding and clear distinction between practice-led research, practice-based research and question-led research, and the contextual significance of each, as well as enabling the reader to comprehend the historical relationships between academic disciplines and the value of reconnecting them at an epistemological and philosophical level. We have attempted to achieve this via the integration of several varied and disparate academic disciplines, each of which encapsulates a unique insight into the temporal and contextual significance of epistemology in practice. By integrating specifically selected examples from disciplinary praxis, we hope that readers of the book will be encouraged to develop a capacity not only to think conceptually about the design of their own research, but also to systematically evaluate that of others, through a new critical lens of understanding and inquiry, which paves the way for an enhanced capacity to annotate their researcher positionality and epistemic stance. Our focus on the inclusion of descriptive, exploratory and historical practice is something we hope will serve to inspire, inform and correct often long-held and fundamentally skewed presuppositions of the nature of epistemology and its power to underpin and serve as the potential architect of new knowledge and human understanding. We are hopeful that our approach will foster higher-order critical thinking in relation to methodological implementation, encouraging deep learning processes and the confidence to transcend the limits of one's own discipline, in order to work collaboratively with academic peers and researchers from diverse fields of academic and creative practice, which history has delineated into distinct disciplines that were once irrevocably united by their original ontologies, ideologies and philosophies.

Via this book we have aimed to achieve six fundamentally new things relating to the reconnection of disciplines at an epistemological level, namely:

1) To frame and contextualise the epistemological and philosophical underpinnings of approaches to disciplinary-based research, providing conceptual, contextual and theoretical insight into the process.
2) To develop an understanding of the distinctions between practice-led research, practice-based research and question-led research, acknowledging the contextual significance of each.
3) To enable comprehension of the historical relationships between academic disciplines and the value of reconnecting each, at an epistemological and philosophical level.
4) To provide a strategic focus of descriptive, exploratory and experimental studies from practice; and to foster higher-order critical thinking in relation to methodological implementation in research.

5) To encourage deep learning processes which underpin confidence in transcending the limits of one's own discipline in order to work collaboratively with researchers in parallel or alternative fields.
6) To use integrated examples from specific disciplines to consider the conceptual and contextual bases of epistemology that continue to shape academic and research-based praxis.

Our specific focus on the notion of transdisciplinarity in the book has stemmed from our facilitation of postgraduate students, many of whom are already established in their own communities of professional practice when they arrive to undertake doctoral- or masters-level programmes. We recognise that the capacity of our students to develop and progress ultimately necessitates focus on the development of higher-order critical thinking skills, and a proactive approach to challenging the inertia of organisational infrastructures, cultures and settings. It is the capacity to demonstrate these characteristics which ultimately leads to the establishment of "doctoralness" in the ability of students to conceptualise and theorise at an appropriate academic threshold level.

Delineating academic disciplinarity

Certainly, in more empirical sciences, postmodernism has ensured that processes of research design and methodology have increasingly become characterised by the systematisation and logic of recognised academic disciplines. In health and medicine, for example, this has been further compounded by the concept of evidence-based practice and the need to legitimise, rationalise and make tangible research outputs. This progressive delineation in academic disciplinarity has led to a progressive disconnect in the historically recognisable epistemologies that once shaped very disparate disciplines.

At an epistemological level, research in arts and social sciences has a longstanding shared origin but, consequently, an often disparate approach to implementation in the creation and acquisition of new knowledge. In turn, these impact on how research is interpreted, disseminated and deemed as relevant in the context of discipline-specific research. It can be debated that this conceptual dichotomy can be used as a means of widening the appreciation of discipline-specific approaches to research methodology and can provide the academic staff supervising postgraduate students at doctoral and masters levels with a greater level of conceptual and theoretical underpinning, which will ultimately enhance their capacity for critical thinking and perhaps, more importantly, for the transcendence of disciplinarity between the signature pedagogies represented globally in higher education and research institutions.

The evaluative capacity of all research students is pivotal in their ability to frame and contextualise their own work in the global research arena. The subtleties of difference at a philosophical level can have a dramatic impact on the overall outcome of research execution. There is a need for this to be made explicit in the published literature available to academic staff and students in the conceptual framing of their contributions to applied professional practice, regardless of professional discipline.

We have aimed to ensure that this book is presented as a means of comprehensively grounding and considering epistemological approaches to research. We believe this has been achieved through the integration of praxis-based examples from history and the reconnection of their relevance to contemporaneous professional practice. This provides an opportunity for readers to challenge their own approaches to the development of their own higher-order critical thinking in relation to methodological implementation, with a specific focus on descriptive, exploratory and experimental studies from practice. At the level of methods, the illumination of shared approaches to data collection, analysis, interpretation and dissemination processes provide an insight into the potential of these to positively impact on research execution.

We are hopeful that this book will not only introduce students to the diverse array of epistemological tools and concepts necessary to underpin their own postgraduate research, but also to a wider capacity for conceptual thinking, which will serve to increase their intellectual understanding as well as giving them an appreciation for their work as a natural progression from, and direct consequence of, their historical peers.

We hope too that this book will serve as a valuable text for postgraduate educators, who might use it to consolidate and support their own knowledge in the support of students seeking to make substantial, or even fundamentally unique, contributions to knowledge.

The book editors and chapter authors have all been identified as academics who can authentically contribute to the aim of illuminating the reconnection of disparate epistemological approaches and, as such, have provided an insight into their own professional disciplines. Professor Kevin Petrie has worked to provide a unique series of accompanying abstract artworks as a means of symbolically representing the historical epistemologies identified throughout the book with their contemporaneous counterparts from applied practice. We hope that these illustrations might provide a source of contemplation for readers as they reflect on their own understanding of positional stance in relation to the establishment of ontologies and epistemologies.

Navigating this book is very straightforward in that we have designed it to be read as either a whole text or as a series of individual chapters, so that areas of specific interest can quickly be identified. Wherever possibly, we have cross-referenced other chapters which may be of direct relevance to that which is being read, and we hope this will make the book more accessible to those whose interest in epistemology might be relatively new, as well as serving as a valuable adjunct work for those more experienced in the discipline.

Professor Catherine Hayes
June 2020

1
DEFINING AND FRAMING EPISTEMOLOGY

Catherine Hayes and Peter Smith

But epistemology is always and inevitably personal. The point of the probe is always in the heart of the explorer: What is my answer to the question of the nature of knowing?

Gregory Bateson (1972)

Introduction

As alluded to by the quotation above, in the context of the paradigmatic sufficiency of social research, epistemology is an integral component in the relationship between ontology, philosophy, methodology and methods. This chapter will provide an overview of epistemology in the context of knowledge and knowledge acquisition in the context of this relationship. An insight will be gained into the relative differences that can exist between different types of knowledge and how these then influence how knowledge is established, articulated and regarded in the wider context of research.

We operationally define epistemology, within this chapter, as the nature and form of knowledge with regard to how their relationship is articulated in practice. Underpinning our definition is the assumption that the basis of all human knowledge is subjective and is rooted in the socially constructed meaning-making that underpins human curiosity, inquiry and, subsequently, assumption. The context of social science presents an ideal arena from a disciplinary perspective to consider the relationship between what it is actually possible to know and the knower.

What this relationship actually constitutes is a prevailing dilemma in the study of epistemology that has been continually extended to incorporate the concept of the personal in epistemic cognition. That dilemma is the notion of perceived versus actual reality and whether a re-examination of the constructive alignment of methodological approaches to social research is required.

The acquisition of knowledge in relation to sensory engagement with specific artefacts (like art) or media (such as music) presents an alternative insight into what knowledge actually is, especially in contrast to the study of propositional knowledge or truth in the social sciences. It is here that we posit how the relative inseparability of cognitive skill and affective impact are evident, and where the concept of aesthetic knowledge is open to question in terms of the internalisation of perceived reality. In turn, this raises questions of what actually constitutes knowledge or whether knowledge itself can be perceived in the context of sensory engagement – a process of critical reflection which can potentially lead to critical reflexivity in action. Academic researchers doubtlessly use reflection to challenge their personally held assumptions and translate this into deliberate action in the real world – as with seminal academic texts, such as the work of Shakespeare, the universality of creative practice has the potential to transcend generations and become an embedded part of historical knowledge, capturing an insight into our cultural heritage and ancestry (Stupples, 2017).

While art does not seek or necessitate propositional truth in the same sense as evidence-based approaches to health and social care, we posit that it provides a metaphorical anchor for the recognition that all interpretation is essentially subjective, when perceived and reported by humankind. Ultimately, all ways of knowing, regardless of discipline, have the capacity to shape how sense is made of the world within which we exist. As such, it can be stated that all epistemological stances are beyond disciplinarity, and it is the methodological approaches that define our signature and traditionally adopted methods in the acquisition of knowledge in practice.

Gaining an insight into the liminal space between what is the basis of knowing and the knower is essential to deconstructing meaning in the context of perception (Fox, 2017). This insight can then be used to consider how personal epistemology influences choice of philosophical underpinnings in processes of research design and methodology. By facilitating the consideration of both traditional and contemporary epistemological lenses, using recognised philosophical perspectives, it is possible to raise awareness of a wider range of epistemological stances. Making sense is an integral part of being human (Eisner, 2017). It lies at the heart of the fundamental understanding, explanation and comprehension (Park, 2017). In terms of human need, control of extraneous environments and the emotions that regulate interaction with them are the pivotal basis of the need to "make sure". This has now also become a core characteristic in how tacit knowledge can become transferrable knowledge in the context of gamification (ter Vrugte and de Jong, 2017). Basically, it implies that the relationship between the human mind and the universe in which it is acknowledged to exist is pivotal to knowledge and subsequent understanding.

Contextualising and framing epistemology

Epistemology extends beyond the scope of purist philosophy, which is significant in how it effectively reaches beyond the context of disciplinarity in social research. Epistemology is not only an academic endeavour; it is pivotal in the transgenerational sharing of knowledge from one to the next, where knowledge rather than perception ultimately underpins belief (Kaplan, Sanchez and Hoffman, 2017).

Justifying or providing an evidence base for knowledge is now a fundamental part of social science research. It is the basis of rationalism, empiricism and the fundamental structure of knowledge. The concept of perceived versus actual reality is important in differentiating what we perceive knowledge to be from what it is. The differentiation between what knowledge is and what knowledge actually constitutes is also paramount, since it impacts on the capacity that humankind has to react to it in practice (Carter, 2017).

It ought to be acknowledged, too, that many individuals embody or espouse an absolutist perspective and that a more evaluative perspective of different domains of knowledge in social research is necessary in practice (Markauskaite and Goodyear, 2017). In this chapter, we contemplate both theoretical and practical considerations, using examples from both creative arts practice and qualitative social sciences to illustrate how the basis of epistemological thinking can be used to underpin the methodology of practice-based research and its subjective evaluation.

The inextricable link between ontology and epistemology

Where theoretical positioning illuminates the whole rationale for social research, the significance of ontology and epistemology is irrefutable (Cunliffe and Scaratti, 2017). An understanding of each and, in particular, their embedded and symbiotic relationship is essential in subsequently understanding the connection between the origins and foundations of research. The morphologic design of research is dependent on the ontological and epistemological stances underpinning it and which then support the adoption of specific methodologies and methods. Certain ontological and epistemological stances offer the opportunity for the researcher to acknowledge their own embedded stance or philosophical assumptions, which could potentially influence researchers' interpretive capacity and ability to disseminate findings in the context of social research methods.

Ontology

The term ontology can be operationally defined with respect to its relationship with epistemology. Essentially, two distinct ontological positions exist: foundationalism and anti-foundationalism. Both deal with the nature of being, truth and reality. It is the theoretical significance of ontology that embeds it into the very being of an epistemological stance.

Foundationalism posits that the reality of the world exists in the form of a mosaic, composed of the material substances of a physical world. These materials are extraneous and independent of the human experience. Anti-foundationalism in contrast posits that there can be nothing independent of knowledge, since social construction of the world by human actors is what gives them their meaning, sense-making and ultimately their reality (Spiegel, 2017).

Foundationalism and anti-foundationalism, as the two most prominent ontological stances, frame and determine the epistemological stance or "ways of knowing". Most commonly associated with the two distinctions in ontological stance are: (a) empirical or positivist epistemology (the notion that world reality exists value free and independently of human knowledge of it); and (b) subjective or interpretivist epistemology (which posits that there is a social construction of the work that has engendered meaning and subjectivity).

The illumination of subjective interpretation can therefore be regarded as a double hermeneutic, which negates the need for objectivity in the construction of new theoretical perspectives. The objective entity represented by the world means it is possible to generate specific questions or hypotheses which can be tested by direct observation. In this sense, there is an evidently parallel position with natural science, which also uses theoretical perspectives in order to generate new hypotheses that can be tested by direct observation as well.

If these suppositions hold, it is possible to state that the world itself represents an objective entity, which can subsequently be subject to verification and further investigation. Differentiating the aim of explaining action rather than the meaning of it is what characterises positivist inquiry. The interpretivist stance stands in contrast to this, positing that without perceived reality, things cannot exist. It is from this stance that interpretivist research seeks the multiple subjective realities of those experiencing specific phenomena.

Methodological alignment

There is an evident and frequently reported constructive alignment between ontology, epistemology, philosophy, methodology and methods (Choi and Richards, 2017). With this alignment, it is possible to see the assumed precedence of each in the context of social research. There is inevitably an assumed resultant methodological stance that results as a direct consequence of differing ontological or epistemological origin. The collective consideration of all five is essential in the context of social research if there is to be a degree of systematisation of emergent theoretical perspectives.

Since a dichotomy can exist between ontological and epistemological stances, it is possible to have alternative resultant views of the same phenomena in research. There is a functional dependence rather than a hierarchical sense of precedence between ontology, epistemology, philosophy, methodology and methods, and it is this which provides an overarching means of knowing the world and developing universal understanding of it.

Within a different signature discipline, art and creative practice provide an opportunity for new knowledge development and the making of the essential beliefs and values that people project onto tangible objects or phenomena that act as foci for the development of cognition and epistemological understanding. The authors' differing disciplinary perspectives and signature pedagogies make these an ideal choice of discussion. In terms of their applied practical relevance, they clearly illustrate characteristics of epistemological approaches in practice.

In terms of operationally defining a philosophical standpoint, we posit that this is where the interpretivist stance aligns with knowledge in the context of applied practice. It moves epistemology or ways of knowing from a process of transactional gain to one of facilitation of inherent belief (Alvesson and Sköldberg, 2009). The epistemology of perception is such that the psychological or cognitive impact of art and creative practice is permitted visibility and resonance. Linked to this is the evocation of cognitive capacity, the potential for experience to add to epistemic cognition and the foundation of the debate as to whether cognitive and affective capacities are truly inseparable (Hasan, 2017).

These affective/emotive standpoints are pivotal to any consideration of creative practice since they facilitate the theoretical embedding of social constructionism or situate it in broader contexts of our human thought (Brown, 2017).

The conceptual common denominator in this process is cognition and it is at this point that the question of where human epistemology sits relative to human cognition is significant. Ayn Rand's (1990) response to this was to note that humans' cognitive faculty is conceptual, which again stems back to the nature of truth and knowledge (ontology).

Metaphysics embraces this context and is embedded in metacognition to form what is commonly termed epistemic cognition. From a metaphysical perspective, art posits or evokes emotion and hence art becomes a means of making tangible metaphysics in the form of objects or specific phenomena (Kitchner, 1983).

Integrating conceptual knowledge and the notion of perceived reality

The integration of conceptual knowledge with sense data facilitates how visual abstractions can be directly linked to cognition. This is framed in the conceptual designation or delivery of cognate mechanisms where sensory perception begins and ends, for example via the eyes, touch sensors in the skin, the ears or in the nose, in relation to our ability to smell (Eisner, 2017). It can be posited that every living individual possesses their own perceived reality of the world, which can be regarded as subjective truth (Bruce and Young, 1998).

Essentially, there are four aspects of human experience which are of significance to the epistemic cognition:

- Corporeality, which alludes to the notion of lived bodily experiences
- Spatiality, which considers the concept of lived space
- Relationality, which is directly concerned with lived human relationships
- Temporality, which is an engagement with the concept of lived time

As a consequence of these four aspects, methodologically speaking, the only reliable person to disseminate the reality of lived experience is the subject. Understanding human behaviour and experience requires the person to interpret the action or experience from the researcher; then the researcher must interpret the explanation provided by the person (Miščević, 2017). It is the most significant emotionally charged aspects of reality concept formation that characterise question-led research, since all inquiry, however empirical, still has to stem from human inquiry and human curiosity (Jiménez, 2017). The significance of the phenomena is also important since it entails the selective recreation of objective reality rather than the metaphysical assumptions surrounding it at an epistemic level (Pollner, 1975).

The concept of tacit versus rational knowledge construction

In the 21st century, knowledge construction and evolution no longer remain in distinct disciplinary silos. From the evolution of information technology (IT) has emerged a culture where, at a pragmatic level and to varying different degrees, knowledge is characterised by its relative degrees of disciplinarity, interdisciplinarity, multidisciplinarity or transdisciplinarity (Kreber, 2010). All of these concepts necessitate a consideration of the contextual or situational status of knowledge in relation to its potential for transferability and translation from theory to praxis, and how this impacts on traditional boundaries of "knowing" for each respective discipline.

The notion of professionalising knowledge came as a direct consequence of a need to maintain a rigid, professional stance in the earlier days of established professions such as medicine and law (Barbaro-Brown, 2013). Disciplinary knowledge-sharing is focused and, within the context of the social sciences, has often been risk averse in approaches to creativity and innovation (Klemm, 2017).

Communities of practice have become the socially contextualised versions of knowledge and where it is housed (Guldberg, 2017). Knowledge has often been posited as elitist, exclusive and limited by the ethics of professions, where status level elevated them to the extent that newly generated knowledge had to be exclusive, revered and largely inaccessible to the wider world. With the IT emergence, this changed; knowledge that would simply not have been shared is now freely available for download from the internet (Barnett and Bengtsen, 2017). As a result of this, the majority of knowledge, while having a strong disciplinary knowledge foundation, is now open for the integration of creation, innovation and the transcendence of application in practice (Olson and Brosnan, 2017). Where tensions between theory and practice are is usually the liminal basis for large-scale and often divided opinion as to where knowledge actually originates from and is presently framed and contextualised (Seremani and Clegg, 2016).

However, where knowledge is impossible and impractical to categorise and rationalise, then the hierarchy of where this sits societally means that much of the theoretical backdrop to creative practice is little discussed in alternative forms, because of its lack of capacity for a strategic fit with the concept of evidence-based practice, testifiability and generalisability. Added to this are the situational complexity of delivery and the lack of willingness to extend and develop academic curricula beyond the confines of individual disciplinarity (Hatleskog, Holder and Hoete, 2016).

How academics and students behave as professionals is ultimately directed by the teaching methodologies underpinning their education (Cruess, Cruess and Steinert, 2016). An introduction of inquiry-based learning and student-centred delivery in traditionally didactic subject areas has meant a switch to informal social constructivist philosophy, which lends itself much more clearly to creative arts practice and thinking in action (McIntyre and Coffee, 2016).

Where the commodification of education in recent years is part of this, via performance measures of what mainly constitutes employability in the future, is evident (Hall and Smyth, 2016). Roberts and Codd (2010) clearly identified the core and anecdotal basis of neoliberalism in 21st-century educational delivery as the rigid staunch adherence to learning outcomes and the objectification of knowledge, so misaligned with the concepts of creativity and adaptive intelligence that typically characterise a professional learner. The dissonance of pedagogy and the popularisation or fashionability of knowledge is also a key issue for development in educational settings, where the context and nature of knowledge development is fundamental to the ethos of learning (Farrelly, Shapiro and Tomaš, 2017).

In order to explore how we move "beyond disciplinarity" from an epistemological stance, it is first necessary to explore where the different origins or homes of disciplinarity determine how they are contextualised and framed today. The emergence of contemplative pedagogies in the healthcare sciences, for example, has changed perceptions of knowing – though not so much for empirical sciences such as chemistry, due to the contextual restraints of laboratory work and a more rationalised need for deductive models and, to a certain extent, an advocation of binary thinking. Disciplines such as nursing have a more relative stance, primarily because they work with people, where social interactivity lies at the heart of caring and compassionate healthcare practice (Kaufman, 2017).

The last decade of educational policy has seen a clearly demarcated shift to the integration of work-based learning opportunities and the notion that transferrable skills somehow usurp disciplinary knowledge and the paradigms that underpin its development (Whitehead, 2013; Richard, 2012; Wolf 2011). The fact that we equip people for society and not for a role descriptor is evidently lost in the midst of the neoliberalist commodification of tacit knowledge-makers. It is here that the legitimacy of knowledge in the creative arts is paralleled by a shift in healthcare in becoming evidence-based (Burke and Onsman, 2017; Stevens et al., 2017). This has in itself been rooted in domain specificity, rather than the embodiment of what someone is actually good at because of their innate psychomotor, cognitive or affective skills (Baer, 2017).

The contested nature of knowledge was a 20th-century phenomenon. In moving beyond disciplinarity it is pivotal, therefore, that new discourse is aligned with all signature pedagogies, but situated socially and contextually (Rochberg, 2017).

The social realist stance adopted by Bernstein (2000) is rooted in the social construction of knowledge. Broad distinctions between not just what is known, but also how, dominate discussions where the value of practical and applied skills can be characterised by context-specific knowledge. Capacity for collaborative or co-construction of knowledge is also a significant feature of the creation of new knowledge. Ensuring a generic approach to how students fit into and contribute to civic responsibility upon completion of the first phase of their undergraduate education is geared to a far greater extent to the concept of voluntary service in practice – citizenship in action (McIlrath, 2017). Sociocultural perspectives and traditions in art and creative practice ensure this. Impact and neoliberalist perspectives do not always go hand in hand. Authentic pedagogies are demonstrated where professionals are embedded with real-life practical skills. Synergies beyond disciplinarity therefore have the potential to be contrived, tokenistic and self-indulgent in relation to whoever exacts them in practice and the situational context of this (Choi and Richards, 2017).

Creative practice and art maintain their conceptual importance because of their originality – this can be posited as a literal truth that, in terms of psycho-epistemological function, necessitates an ongoing capacity for human perception. It also establishes the need for receptivity and self-sufficiency on behalf of the interpreter (Muis and Franco, 2010). The more complex and abstract a piece of artwork is, the less it is readily recognisable, which in terms of challenging assumptions in the epistemology of social science is highly relative, creating an active dissonance between art and social science at an epistemological level (Blackman, 2017). It is the concept of embedded abstraction which has the capability of conveying the unknown. A key example of this is stained-glass window storytelling in theology. The integration of conceptual knowledge into sense data is a fundamental part of this.

Chagall's focus on how art can provide the vehicle for driving prayer for redemption typifies this illustration. Through biblical storytelling, stained glass can, through its creation, not only metaphorically represent the fracture of Christ's body, but can, through its medium, also metaphorically and physically represent the light and hope associated with his resurrection. Richter posited that art was the "highest form of hope". Heidegger posited that art, rooted in the notion of "truth", was its ultimate embodiment. Stained-glass windows of theology represent one mechanism of bridging the gap between communal connection and individual engagement with faith (Paige, 2016).

Traditional and contemporary epistemological lenses

The focus on certainty, binary thinking and absolute perspectives is characterised nowhere better than in the work of Karl Popper, who asserted that no general truth can ever be known about the world with absolute certainty. His work in the context of scientific inquiry exerted a huge influence on 20th-century approaches to research (Popper, 2013). His key point is that we cannot know any general truth about the world for sure. Since we can only directly observe a finite number of phenomena or events, we cannot guarantee certainly or absolutely that our propositions may not be challenged (Russell, 1912). Popper thus asserted that the pursuit of new knowledge always emanates from the need to falsify or contradict the extant evidence base to date. In terms of falsification, the more we cannot falsify something, the more we have the right to claim certainty about certain phenomena. Falsifying something then necessitates the development of an alternative theory or perspective; therefore, all empirical research in cognate disciplines ought to be open to critical appraisal and the possibility of refutation or contradiction (Holtz and Monnerjahn, 2017).

Philosophical stance and ways of knowing

The capacity for reasoning and defence lies at the heart of propositional knowledge – the debate as to whether misrepresentation could potentially become a source of great concern. Klinke (2014) highlights how Plato's "Allegory of the cave" describes a system of epistemology in which there are three stages of understanding – from interpreting mere shadows, to understanding that these are shadows only and grasping the ideas behind the apparent world. For Plato, those ideas, not the material world, are the highest forms of reality and constitute real knowledge (Klinke, 2014).

Critical reflection and the capacity for reflexivity in the context of decision-making now characterises the majority of medical and allied health and social care professions (Kinsella, 2010). This has entrenched the notion of an ethical stance as an integral part of professional practice. This lies in stark contrast to romantic epistemology, which advocates that imagination in conjunction with, and often in preference to, rationalising ways of knowing was the greatest stance. It stems from the notion that accountability in terms of "being" in the world belies the contextual and situational basis of how we might begin to "know" in practice. From this perspective, we posit that it ought to be considered that epistemic reflexivity differs distinctly in terms of context specificity, and that it is this which provides a mechanism of embedding what is epistemically and creatively derived back into processes of institutional approach, politics or technicality (Eisner, 2017).

While creative practice offers no mechanism of addressing empirical truth in relation to the seeking of propositional knowledge, the opportunity to be at one with a representational object offers a means by which the transience of legitimised thoughts can be examined. As such, it necessitates a re-examination of the presuppositions we make about the manner in which we know and gain knowledge from anything non-propositional in nature and presentation.

The concept of a visual epistemology has its origins in the notion of a constructed and idealised mental imagery, which in turn is reflective of the cognitive processes involved in its making. Once translated into a mimetic object, depiction via abstraction is possible, at the heart of which is thinking and creation. As such, the representation of worldviews and life worlds through images remains a contentious debate in the field of visual epistemology and one which can never be confined purely to the discipline of arts and creative practice. This leads clearly into what has been termed "the epistemic potential of pictures" via visual thinking and perception (Klinke, 2014).

In 1781, Kant's *Critique of Pure Reason* provided an insight into how knowledge could be acquired via empirical inquiry and also the relative limitations that seeking to rationalise entails (Kant, 1998). It is the parameters of knowledge and the discernment of what can be known and what can't that epistemology from a disciplinary perspective offers in this context. Kant identified with what he termed empirical experience, which incorporates and embeds all experiences (including those of the senses) in the notion of pre-existing (*a priori*) knowledge, which then has the potential to transform them into concepts which are abstract from consciousness rather than being part of it.

A key example of an approach that focuses on epistemological relativism and illustrates this is Actor Network Theory (ANT), which provides an alternative reflexive lens for examining the subtle difference in the production rather than the discovery of "truth" in empirical inquiry (Latour, 1986). It is a means of recognising and segregating epistemic cognition, since it permits actors to define the world "in their own terms" (Latour, 1999). Whittle and Spicer's (2008) insight into ANT shows that, whether intentional or not, ANT's ethnocentrism (as highlighted by Bloomfield and Vurdubakis, 1999) implies that participant explanations are at best naïve or at worst wrong, which could potentially frame the approach as a grand narrative (Lee and Brown 1994). To be truly reflexive, though, necessitates a value-laden approach to all perceived realities having intrinsic truth.

Beyond disciplinarity in ways of knowing

Interaction with social objects is inherently value laden, but also necessitates cognitive engagement in the process of making meaning and internalising perceived and actual experience. In aesthetics, this has several implications for an epistemological stance, in that it has the capacity to fundamentally alter how we make sense of things and how we then translate sense-making into action as a result of our epistemic cognition. There are two types of practice-related research which can be operationally defined: (a) practice-based (if a creative artefact is the basis of the contribution to knowledge, the research is practice-based); and (b) practice-led (if the research leads primarily to new understandings about practice, it is practice-led).

It is here that propositional content is debated. Historically, the debate of whether knowledge can emerge from a social object is fraught with division in relation to the notion of propositional language, insight and reflection. This is embedded in the notion and seeking of truth (Platts, 2016). What is not tangible is the knowledge that art imparts, but rather the impact of it. Dimensionality and interdisciplinary difference is a fundamental consideration of what knowledge is and what it informs.

Shared epistemological stance in social research

Social sciences require that particular epistemological reflections be approached from characteristic theoretical developments and empirical research practice. Such reflections that are present in scientists' practical activity, even though they may not be named as such, are closely linked with the elucidation of the paradigms in force in the production of every discipline. We define those paradigms as the theoretical-methodological framework used by researchers to interpret social phenomena in the context of a given society.

As a result of epistemological reflection on social sciences in general, and sociology in particular, I conclude that there are three main co-existing paradigms, two of them already established: the historical materialistic and the positivist ones, and a third paradigm – the interpretive one – which is on its way to being a more and more unquestioned consolidation. Such paradigms, emerging from established theoretical perspectives, have different ontological, epistemological and, consequently, methodological assumptions; so much so that evolution or reflection produced in one of them is not applicable as such to the others. Likewise, those paradigms are, more often than not, at the basis of the interpretive models used by the speakers to describe social reality.

Conclusion

Our consideration of epistemology as a conduit between ontology and methodology has provided an insight into how this is shared within the context of "ways of knowing" across arts and social science research. The recognition that at an epistemological level, social science and creative practice/art are on the same continuum, attests to the fact that both represent attempts to make sense and meaning of the external world. This highlights the contested nature of reason and development in both. Epistemology raises several core questions of how reality can really be known; the relationship between the knower and the known; and characteristics and principles that guide the process of knowing. Unlike epistemology, epistemological reflection does not seek universality or generalisability. It is on the basis of universality that epistemological reflection and epistemology in social science empirical research practice fluctuates and elucidates the different paradigms – which, in turn, provide different answers to the questions raised, given that sciences do not.

In reconnecting ways of knowing and alluding to interdisciplinarity and transdisciplinarity, there is a risk of being tokenistic in how these can become operational in practice. A clear mechanism of seeing where "how we know" becomes an embedded part of "why we know" ultimately determines both tacit and rational knowledge. This provides both challenges and opportunities to reconnect disparate signature disciplines at an epistemological level. This subsequently has implications for the execution of research design and methodology, and how individual disciplinary perspectives in the arts and social sciences are perceived and represented. Transcending disciplinarity is becoming a pivotal part of the overarching strategic approach of knowledge-producing institutions, such as universities and learned institutions and societies, and this chapter has provided an overview of key considerations of relevance to operationalising approaches to it.

References

Alvesson, M & Sköldberg, K (2009). *Reflexive Methodology: New Vistas for Qualitative Research* (2nd ed.). Thousand Oaks, CA: Sage.

Baer, J (2017). Content matters: Why nurturing creativity is so different in different domains. In RA Beghetto & B Sriraman (Eds). *Creative Contradictions in Education: Cross Disciplinary Paradoxes and Perspectives* (pp.129–140). Cham, Switzerland: Springer International Publishing.

Barbaro-Brown J (2013). Professional identity: Who do we think we are? In C Hayes (Ed.). *Professional Practice for Podiatric Medicine*. Keswick, UK: M&K Update Ltd. (pp.1–16)

Barnett, R & Bengtsen, S (2017). Universities and epistemology: From a dissolution of knowledge to the emergence of a new thinking. *Education Sciences*, 7(1), 38.

Bateson, G (1972). *Steps to an Ecology of Mind: Collected Essays in Anthropology, Psychiatry, Evolution, and Epistemology*. Chicago: University of Chicago Press.

Bernstein, BB (2000). *Pedagogy, Symbolic Control, and Identity: Theory, Research, Critique (No. 4)*. Lanham, MD: Rowman & Littlefield.

Blackman, RR (2017). Education, exhibition, and publication as predictors of success in the art world: A study of selected participants in the Whitney Biennial, 1989 to 2008. Doctoral dissertation, n.p.

Bloomfield, BP & Vurdubakis, T (1999). The outer limits: Monsters, actor networks and the writing of displacement. *Organization*, 6(4), 625–647.

Brown, NCM (Ed.) (2017). *Studies in Philosophical Realism in Art, Design and Education*. Cham, Switzerland: Springer International Publishing.

Bruce, V & Young, A (1998). *In the Eye of the Beholder: The Science of Face Perception*. Oxford: Oxford University Press.

Burke, R & Onsman, A (2017). Discordant methodologies: Prioritizing performance in artistic research in music. In R Burke & A Onsman (Eds). *Perspectives on Artistic Research in Music* (pp.3–17). Lanham, MD: Lexington Books.

Carter, JA (2017). Epistemological implications of relativism. In JJ Ichikawa (Ed.). *The Routledge Handbook of Epistemic Contextualism* (pp.292–302). Abingdon, UK: Routledge.

Choi, S & Richards, K (2017). Understanding interdisciplinarity. In S Choi & K Richards (Eds). *Interdisciplinary Discourse* (pp.39–69). Basingstoke, UK: Palgrave Macmillan UK.

Cruess, RL, Cruess, SR & Steinert, Y (2016). Amending Miller's pyramid to include professional identity formation. *Academic Medicine, 91*(2), 180–185.

Cunliffe, AL & Scaratti, G (2017). Embedding impact in engaged research: Developing socially useful knowledge through dialogical sensemaking. *British Journal of Management, 28*(1), 29–44.

Eisner, EW (2017). *The Enlightened Eye: Qualitative Inquiry and the Enhancement of Educational Practice*. New York: Teachers College Press.

Farrelly, R, Shapiro, S & Tomaš, Z (2017). Creating the conditions for productive dissonance: An inclusive pedagogical framework. In A Lee & RD Williams (Eds). *Engaging Dissonance: Developing Mindful Global Citizenship in Higher Education* (pp.25–42). Bingley, UK: Emerald Publishing Limited.

Fox, HM (2017). A way of knowing in search of our true identity. *Self & Society, 45*(1), 72–75.

Guldberg, K (2017). Enhancing the impact of research and knowledge co-production in higher education through communities of practice. In J McDonald & A Cater-Steel (Eds). *Communities of Practice: Facilitating Social Learning in Higher Education* (pp.261–278). Singapore: Springer Singapore.

Hall, R & Smyth, K (2016). Dismantling the curriculum in higher education. *Open Library of Humanities, 2*(1), 4–29.

Hasan, A (2017). *A Critical Introduction to the Epistemology of Perception*. London: Bloomsbury Publishing.

Hatleskog, E, Holder, A & Hoete, A (2016). Talking architecture: Exploring knowledge production through conversation in architectural creative practice research. *Networking Knowledge: Journal of the MeCCSA Postgraduate Network, 9*(3). https://doi.org/10.31165/nk.2016.93.437

Holtz, P & Monnerjahn, P (2017). Falsificationism is not just "potential" falsifiability, but requires "actual" falsification: Social psychology, critical rationalism, and progress in science. *Journal for the Theory of Social Behaviour, 47*(3), 348–362.

Jiménez, AC (2017). How knowledge grows: An anthropological anamorphosis. In J Shaffner & H Wardle (Eds). Cosmopolitics (pp.227–264). Fife, UK: Open Anthropology Cooperative Press.

Kant, I (1998). *Critique of Pure Reason* (trans. P Guyer & AW Wood). Cambridge: Cambridge University Press.

Kaplan, M, Sanchez, M & Hoffman, J (2017). *Intergenerational Pathways to a Sustainable Society*. Cham, Switzerland: Springer International Publishing.

Kaufman, P (2017). Critical contemplative pedagogy. *Radical Pedagogy, 14*(1). 1–20.

Kinsella, EA (2010). Professional knowledge and the epistemology of reflective practice. *Nursing Philosophy, 11*(1), 3–14.

Kitchner, KS (1983). Cognition, metacognition, and epistemic cognition. *Human Development, 26*(4), 222–232.

Klemm, WR (2017). Leadership and creativity. In J Marques & S Dhiman (Eds). *Leadership Today: Practices for Personal and Professional Performance* (pp.263–278). Cham, Switzerland: Springer International Publishing.

Klinke, H (Ed.). (2014). *Art Theory as Visual Epistemology*. Newcastle upon Tyne, UK: Cambridge Scholars Publishing.

Kreber, C (2010). *The University and Its Disciplines: Teaching and Learning Within and Beyond Disciplinary Boundaries.* Abingdon, UK: Routledge.

Latour, B (1986). Visualization and cognition. *Knowledge and Society, 6*(6), 1–40.

Latour, B (1999). On recalling ANT. *The Sociological Review, 47*(S1), 15–25.

Lee, N & Brown, S (1994). Otherness and the actor network: The undiscovered continent. *American Behavioral Scientist, 37*(6), 772–790.

Markauskaite, L & Goodyear, P (2017). *Epistemic Fluency and Professional Education: Innovation, Knowledgeable Action and Actionable Knowledge.* Dordrecht, The Netherlands: Springer Netherlands.

McIlrath, L. (2017). The civic university: A legal and policy vacuum? In J Sachs & L Clark (Eds). *Learning Through Community Engagement: Vision and Practice in Higher Education* (pp. 17–29). Singapore: Springer Singapore.

McIntyre, P & Coffee, S (2016). The arts and design: From romantic doxa to rational systems of creative practice. In P McIntyre, J Fulton & E Paton (Eds). *The Creative System in Action: Understanding Cultural Production and Practice* (pp. 185–199). Basingstoke, UK: Palgrave Macmillan UK.

Miščević, N (2017). Epistemic value, curiosity, knowledge and response-dependence. *Croatian Journal of Philosophy, 16*(3(48)), 393–418.

Muis, KR & Franco, GM (2010). Epistemic profiles and metacognition: Support for the consistency hypothesis. *Metacognition and Learning, 5*(1), 27–45.

Olson, RE & Brosnan, C (2017). *Examining Interprofessional Education Through the Lens of Interdisciplinarity: Power, Knowledge and New Ontological Subjects.* London: Minerva.

Paige, MMJ (2016). Professions of faith: Stained glass making and the visual culture of theology. Doctoral dissertation, University of Stirling.

Park, CL (2017). Distinctions to promote an integrated perspective on meaning: Global meaning and meaning-making processes. *Journal of Constructivist Psychology, 30*(1), 14–19.

Platts, M (2016). *Reference, Truth and Reality: Essays on the Philosophy of Language.* Basingstoke, UK: Routledge.

Pollner, M (1975). "The very coinage of your brain": The anatomy of reality disjunctures. *Philosophy of the Social Sciences, 5*(3), 411–430.

Popper, K (2013). *Realism and the Aim of Science: From the Postscript to the Logic of Scientific Discovery.* Basingstoke, UK: Routledge.

Rand, A (1990). *Introduction to Objectivist Epistemology (Expanded Second Edition).* New York: Penguin.

Richard, D (2012). *The Richard Review of Apprenticeships.* London: BIS.

Roberts, P & Codd, J (2010). Neoliberal tertiary education policy. In M Thrupp & R Irwin (Eds). Another Decade of New Zealand Education Policy: Where to Now? (pp. 99–110). Hamilton, New Zealand: School of Education, University of Waikato.

Rochberg, F (2017). *Before Nature: Cuneiform Knowledge and the History of Science.* Chicago: University of Chicago Press.

Russell, B (1912). What is logic? In JG Slater (Ed.) (1992). *The Collected Papers of Bertrand Russell. Volume 6: Logical and Philosophical Papers, 1909–13* (pp. 54–56). London: Routledge

Seremani, TW & Clegg, S (2016). Postcolonialism, organization, and management theory: The role of "epistemological third spaces". *Journal of Management Inquiry, 25*(2), 171–183.

Spiegel,TJ (2017). Naturalism, quietism and the concept of nature. In M Gyöngyösi, Z Kapelner, Z Ádám & I Faragó-Szabó (Eds). On What It Is: Perspectives on Metaphilosophy (pp.47–62). Budapest: Philosophy Workshop of Eötvös József Collegium.

Stevens, KR, Horn, SD, Kean, J, Deshmukh,VG, Mitchell, SA & Nelson, R (2017). Evidence-based practice, practice-based evidence, and health informatics. In R Nelson & N Staggers (Eds). *Health Informatics: An Interprofessional Approach* (pp. 38–59). St Louis, MO: Elsevier.

Stupples, P (2017). Beyond the predicted: Expanding our understanding of creative agency in international development through practice and policy. *International Journal of Cultural Policy, 23*(1), 52–67.

terVrugte, J & de Jong, T (2017). Self-explanations in game-based learning: From tacit to transferable knowledge. In P Wouters (Ed.). *Instructional Techniques to Facilitate Learning and Motivation of Serious Games* (pp.141–159). New York: Springer International Publishing.

Whitehead, N (2013). *Review of Adult Vocational Qualifications in England.* Wath-upon-Dearne, UK: UKCES.

Whittle, A & Spicer, A (2008). Is actor network theory critique? *Organization Studies, 29*(4), 611–629.

Wolf, A (2011). *Review of Vocational Education: The Wolf Report.* London: TSO.

2
REALITY, INSIGHT AND INTERPRETATION WITH MATHEMATICS

Catherine Hayes and Stephen Capper

> *Mathematics, however, is, as it were, its own explanation; this, although it may seem hard to accept, is nevertheless true, for the recognition that a fact is so is the cause upon which we base the proof.*
>
> Girolamo Cardano (1501–1576)

Introduction

In contemplating the epistemological basis of mathematics, it is impossible to ignore the concept of visual thinking. In relation to human understanding and the conceptual basis of research, the discipline has effectively been able to contribute historically to both art and science, more readily than any other purist academic or intellectual field. Not only does mathematics have the capacity to illuminate boundaries of thinking, it has also provided humans with the opportunity of realising the limitations of hypotheses and how traditional and epistemic challenges might be framed. The relationship between the abstract and the visual lies just as much at the heart of fine art as it does in empirical mathematics and, as such, the field represents a perfect opportunity to reintegrate the epistemic thinking and praxis that belie both.

The concept of universality and mathematical design

Theological insights into the potential for a universal creator in line with mathematical design are also the basis of contentious debates as to whether the world we live in and occupy was the result of a great and coincidental cosmic accident known as the "Big Bang", where everything originated from a singularity, or the deliberate mathematical and aesthetic strategic design of God, who ensured the survival of a tiny blue planet amidst the depths of space. Both are entirely valid hypotheses and debating this subject has provided centuries' worth of epistemological and philosophical debate in their own right. It is the consistency of this design, throughout nature and throughout the cosmos, that continues to perplex and intrigue all academic disciplines, from empirically based subjects such as mathematics, physics and astronomy to interpretivist and creatively based subjects such as fine art and design. This chapter seeks to illuminate these debates, and to present the key mathematical epistemologies that take us back into historical eras, where the two were inextricably linked, and also how this link was obscured from evident visibility, but which has been returned to society via a new age of technological advancement.

Core positionality in human epistemology

The relationship, both physical and artistic, between the concepts of the number and artistic design is of longstanding recognition and wonder in the worlds of epistemology, art and science. Design characterises physical reality alongside the interrelationships of numbers, languages and discourses which seek to explain its occurrence in perceived as well as actual reality.

This has had a tangible, yet largely inexplicable, impact on how human research can be regarded as valid and reliable, trustworthy or at all authentic, and has definable components which can reconnect with theology, physics and spirituality – all of which reconnect the human researcher with their core ontologies and the concept of existentialism. It is not the place of this chapter to explain these complex interrelationships, but rather to illuminate their significance to the scale and undertaking that frames and contextualises applied research praxis. There is an irony in that the existential reasoning that permits us to "know" or to have an epistemological basis for reasoning and inquiry also causes us to realise, even more, how much there is yet to be known. Mathematical perspectives can provide something of an insight into this relationship.

The integration of rhetoric into mathematics as a discipline

Ernest (1995) explicated the significance of both rhetoric and justification to the context of mathematics and highlighted the significance of its situated nature in practice, in parallel with Lave and Wenger's (1991) theory of situated learning. This had broad repercussions where, for the first time, people began to formally challenge and make controversial the epistemological nature of mathematics as a discipline, and the potential of it to be absolute in its universality and its capacity to be perfect in the sense of human understanding and application. This broad controversy was termed a fallibilist perspective and generated significant debate, which was ultimately founded on the notion of historical contingency in the latter part of the 20th century (Ernest, 1995).

Meaning-making and intuition with mathematics: Positioning tacit knowledge

The notion that mathematics is an activity of deliberate construction is one where abstracted thinking is inherently limited by individual mathematicians, as they have finite capacity in the infinite context of their abstract thinking. It is firmly linked, too, to issues of temporality and has also been rooted in debates of theology and metaphysics. In this sense, the epistemic nature of mathematics is continually developing. Here, we give an insight into how, as a discipline and a core epistemic subject, mathematics can provide a means of articulating abstraction in the limited physical constraints of contingent objectivity.

Cultural and contextual transcendence and universality of mathematics: Mathematical discourse

Since human civilisation began, its practical reliance on mathematics has transcended language, culture and context. The capacity of humans to annotate both ways of knowing and existence of the human race has ensured that number remains the fundamental mechanism by which our lives are classified in taxonomies that can be used to shape destinies and futures in modern society. The assignation of value enables organisation and systematisation, which subsequently leads to dimensions of number application, such as codifying and encrypting, which now characteristically frame a 21st-century existence.

The perceived complexity of mathematics is framed by its fundamental discourses, which differ significantly in terms of familiar association and use in everyday life. The assignation of symbolic values has defined both wider global and more specifically focused aspects of societal progression, and have consequently shaped historical landscapes. In the context of research, particularly scientific research, the capacity to "rationalise" in a core linguistic sense is to examine the relationships between fundamentally distinct accounts of reality. In this sense, the ambiguity of research across many fields, beyond a scientific basis, is termed a justification or a need, rather than a more purist sense of negotiating what is potentially "reasonable" in practice.

Challenging the parameters of human imagination and cognitive rationalising

Most recently, Abbott (2013) posited that mathematics is no more than the product of human imagination in terms of its epistemic basis, something that has become progressively developed to permit lucid descriptions of reality. Here, Abbot has seminally differentiated between the disciplinary approaches of two distinct but interrelated disciplines of mathematics and engineering. When separated, in terms of philosophical stance, Abbott presents mathematics as a purely "mental construct" or a perceived and theoretical approximation of reality with inherent limitation, because there can be no such thing as mathematical perfection. If this is taken as truth, then the implications of this to human epistemic thinking are significant, since mathematics is simply a product of the cognitive capacity of humans which exists in abstraction from actual reality.

Interrelationships and rudimentary values in the real world

The distinct interrelationship of music and mathematics is one of those areas where disciplinarity transcends beyond the context of language in applied praxis. Within the context of nature, mathematics also transcends human capacity, with several animal species also able to discern and distinguish between rudimentary values. This is fascinating in the sense that it opens the debate as to whether humans invented mathematics or, ultimately, whether it was part of the intelligent design of human beings themselves. Nowhere is this illustrated better than in the Fibonacci sequence.

The Fibonacci sequence is an insight into the fundamental design of nature, and discovery of the sequence brought into relevant debate the concept of design intelligence and its integration and embedding as part of the natural world. When Fibonacci (Leonardo de Pisa), a former accountant turned mathematician, introduced the western world to the advantages of eastern numeracy in the form of decimalisation, it represented a transcendence of core arithmetic and algebra in the Middle Ages. Epistemologically, this had massive implications to western research and was a progenitor of the use of statistical analysis – this work made possible concepts such as tabulation and visual and numerical representation and, as a consequence, increased the degree of accessibility to mathematics by academics in the western world.

The interrelationship of phi and the theological debates of mathematics

The notion of a divine creator is further complicated by the mathematical number 1.618 (phi), named after the Greek sculptor Phidias, who lived around 500 years BCE. His was the first work to use the number as a basis for foundational work in Olympus. Mathematics in relation to both phi and theology is significant in potentially providing evidence of a divine creator, as demonstrated by the authentic reliability of the number throughout the natural world. Theological teaching refers in the book of Genesis to God's creation of the world from nothing (*ex nihilo*). This is reinforced throughout the remainder of the Bible.

> *By the word of the Lord were the heavens made, their starry host by the breath of his mouth.*

> (Psalm 33:6)

It has been posited that the constant number represented by phi could become the embodiment of nothing split into the perfect unity of two parts. It is here that the Fibonacci principle actually converges on 1.618. The relative link to infinity has also been directly connected to the Fibonacci sequence, which essentially becomes the addition of unity to nothingness. Also interlinking with this concept is the notion of a Holy Trinity, where God the Father, God the Son and God the Holy Spirit are one, since exploration of the ratio of every number in the series sees it converging on phi before infinity is reached. Many times this has been termed the "Golden Ratio" and is often regarded as God's signature on the natural world, created from nothing, in aesthetic beauty and union, which – incidentally, or perhaps not so incidentally, depending on our individual faith perspectives – also aligns directly with several scientific explanations of how the universe came into existence via the Big Bang.

Philosophy of mathematics, logic and the foundations of empirical disciplinarity

The philosophy of mathematics as a discipline is inseparable from the concepts of metaphysical reality and epistemology. It has introduced debates of the relevance and perfection of mathematics in both abstract and concrete forms. Whether mathematical entities actually exist beyond a human cognitive realm provides a ready connection for broader philosophical debates rooted in the concepts of existentialism and "being". Where this fundamentally differs in relation to more traditional "ways of knowing" is in the positioning of underpinning perspectives of mathematical logic or rationality. At the heart of this is the debate as to whether specific methods of mathematics actually bear any relation to their underpinning ontological or epistemological basis, or whether they represent a disconnect in the constructive alignment between the two. Progressive thinking since the Renaissance period has led to a gradual resurgence of literature surrounding the epistemological basis of mathematics itself (Shapiro, 2000; Restivo, 2017), all of which has contributed to progressive thinking in this unique discipline.

Mathematics as aesthetics and beauty: Symbolism and number

The issue of creative practice for an artist implies the same degree of aesthetic appreciation yet, in the same manner, artists make something from nothing too. While they may use a diverse array of physical media to facilitate this, it is their creative imagination that is ultimately embodied in new objects and physical artefacts. Their creativity is reflected in the work of mathematicians whose projections also stem from imagination and the potential of theorems – it is here also that the discourse and narrative discourse of symbolism and number can provide artefacts of beauty, which can then be integrated into new perspectives on elegance and beauty.

Many authors posit that mathematics is a rudimentary bridge between art and science which provides a mechanism of epistemically illuminating nature, but one which is not creative in the traditional sense of artistic practice.

The symbolism of mathematics: Knowing by visualisation techniques

The epistemic significance of mathematics in the world now characterises much of what is possible in terms of abstract thinking; in particular, abstract ways of thinking in the empirical sciences and, more specifically, in purist disciplines such as mathematics, physics and chemistry. What constitutes visual thinking is often systematic and logical, especially in relation to being able to imagine, rather than tangibly seeing concepts and the rationality and outcomes of testable hypotheses. How rationalism fits within the realms of imagery, again epistemologically, links the conceptual bases of art and science and challenges us to ask whether mathematics necessarily has to be an empirical discipline when the visual imagination can represent it. The concept of an evidence base in scientific terms is rarely posited in the depths of imagination, but where visual representation in mathematics challenges this epistemic position, it is in the context of the establishment of truth, understanding and the conceptual thinking that defines epistemology as a discipline. The delineation of the capacity for human thought to be rooted, albeit transiently, in diagrammatic as well as symbolic thinking, both triggers the concept of an intuitive response to visual stimulation and, indeed, the basis of what can be termed perceptual reality (Lee and Shin, 2013).

When mathematics moves into the intangible sense of visual representation that cannot be palpably seen, this adds a further degree of ambiguity to the human psyche, which now belies the basis of knowledge and epistemic belief in a universe to which we belong, but can only really estimate the size of in relation to its enormity.

According to Kant (1998) and Gauss (Boniface, 2007), the inseparable link between conceptual thought and human intuition is a historical perspective, rather than a modern-day assumption. Both philosophers' perspectives on pure mathematics posited that without intuitive capacity in the interpretation of outcomes, mathematics as a discipline – in its greatest philosophical and epistemological sense – is meaningless.

Perpetuating clarity via ambiguity

When contemplating the epistemological basis of mathematics and its contribution to human understanding, there are multiple perspectives for consideration. According to Higgins (1998), the concept of mathematical reasoning is commonly associated with the understanding of complex phenomena that can otherwise remain obscure, with mathematics being fundamental to comprehending the facets of their nature and their consequent meaning. This lends itself to the Greek philosopher Plato's epistemological stance, in which knowledge can often be held as a belief that is substantiated with an account or an explanation. However, this theory has historically been challenged throughout the ages by numerous philosophers, none other than Plato himself, who compared mathematical knowledge to knowledge of the good.

Ethics and morality in the epistemology of mathematics

American philosopher James Rachels, who specialised in ethics and animal rights, took the contested standpoint that there are mathematical proofs which are, in their entirety, tangible, whereas the means by which we evidence moral facts are intuitive and without substance, being based predominantly on core values and intuitive responses. However, Hilary Putnam, another American philosopher of mathematics and science, suggested that the concept of moral realism and mathematical realism are no less problematic than each other (Greco and Sosa, 1999; Clarke-Doane, 2014). What this does suggest is that there are a considerable number of stimulating debates to be had around the epistemological basis of mathematics and some of the mysteries surrounding its actual origins. Buldt, Lowe and Muller (2008) postulate that, from a philosophical perspective, mathematics has gained special status in recent times, perhaps in essence due to its supposedly peculiar epistemology, which is said to derive from a special technique referred to as "mathematical proof", and widely accepted figures of speech in 21st-century discourse such as "mathematical precision".

This perspective is largely in keeping with the widely held belief that mathematics is viewed as a special science, one which Buldt et al. (2008) state is one of the few sciences that can lay claim to being able to prove their results through mathematical objectivity, which some sciences can only endeavour to achieve. Moreover, Grattan-Guinness (2004) posits that mathematical statements are either objectively true or false, therefore there should be no disputes surrounding the validity or credibility of its established statements. Prediger (2003) highlights the ontological status of mathematics as a contributing factor to this perspective; mathematical theories have widely been viewed as being conceptually detached from reality, since theories and concepts are explicitly built within a constructed mathematical reality, therefore providing freedom from contestation in the senses of contradiction and refutation. This is in stark contrast to scientific concepts, which are constantly compared to how they correspond with reality in which debate has long prevailed as to whether scientific claims and theories hold their credence.

Scholars have long debated the epistemological differences between mathematics, the arts and natural sciences, with Schroeder (2000) claiming that one of the significant ways in which mathematics differs is in its disconnection from reality and its foundational sociocultural origins and influences, alongside its belief that it is independent of several key elements such as values and time. It is due to these widely held perspectives that mathematics and culture are often perceived to be extremes of each other which are not reconcilable. This is substantiated by Prediger (2003) who observes that the most important difference is in the epistemic status of the disciplines, with some perceiving mathematics as an epistemic exception, contrasting with how natural sciences and arts are viewed due to the profound influences of their cultural and situational backgrounds and contexts.

The contested position of "epistemic exception" has long been debated among academics, and perhaps one way to illuminate the debate around the epistemology of mathematics is to assess one of its greatest mysteries in the Fibonacci numbers and their interrelationship with the Golden Ratio, both of which are said to have a profound influence on many branches of mathematics, aesthetics, art, medicine, engineering, nature, music and economics.

Fibonacci and the interrelationship of the Golden Ratio

The Fibonacci sequence was described by Leonardo de Pisa (nicknamed "Fibonacci"), who suggested that for the integer sequence which starts with 0 or 1, the sequential number is therefore the sum of the two preceding numbers. At the same time, the ratio that is between any given number within a Fibonacci sequence and its predecessor leans towards something referred to as the Golden Ratio or Golden Proportion, which was initially described by Greek mathematician Euclid (Ozturk, Yalta and Yetkin, 2016; Ciucurel, Georgescu and Iconaru, 2018). The Golden Ratio was later discovered by Filius Bonacci to have a numerical value of precisely 1 to 1.61803399, and it was not until the 20th century that the term phi was coined by Mark Barr in commemoration of Greek sculptor Phidias (Alam, Noor, Basri, Yew and Wen, 2015).

According to Iosa, Morone and Paolucci (2018), the Golden Ratio is considered to be the most fascinating number in the history of mathematics and is said to recursively present itself in various facets of human history dating back from the ancient Greeks to the Renaissance period, and to more contemporary scientific and medical research studies. The Fibonacci sequence and Golden Ratio have been subject to numerous inquisitive scholars investigating their existence within a myriad of professional fields such as aesthetics, anthropometry, architecture, arts, physics, biology, physiology, biomechanics, medicine and facial recognition (Ozturk et al., 2016; Iosa et al., 2018; Ciucurel et al., 2018).

Medicine, anatomy and mathematical epistemology

The Fibonacci sequence and the Golden Ratio have been shown to be present within many of the branches of mathematics, including geometry, numerical methods, algebra, matrix theory, classical analysis and spectral analysis, although Adam, Piatek, Pleszczynski, Smolen and Witula (2016) believe that, despite the high level of occurrence, there are still some areas of mathematics that are poorly represented by these two phenomena. In recent years, researchers have shown an increased interest in the relationship between these two complex phenomena and various branches of medicine, with research studies conducted into areas such as cardiovascular systems and blood pressure and physiological, psychological and biomechanical systems, and how they influence the workings of the human body.

According to Ozturk et al. (2016), the cardiovascular system, especially the physical heart, has intrigued researchers regarding its relationship with the Fibonacci sequence and Golden Ratio, primarily due to the harmony and synchrony in which it continuously pumps blood to and from one of the most important organs of the human body. Several studies have been conducted in this area with Ashrafian and Athanasiou (2011) suggesting that, from an anatomical perspective, the number of branches from the vessels of the heart follow the same sequence as stated by Fibonacci and is also analogous to the leaf branching of some trees. Furthermore, they infer that the Fibonacci sequence could be used to develop a novel biomathematical model of the arterial system to potentially predict the geometric and territorial characteristics of coronary heart disease.

In recent years, Yetkin, Sivri, Yalta and Yetkin (2013) have undertaken several research studies regarding the Golden Ratio specific to the heart. They reported data collected from 162 healthy subjects to assess the ratio of cardiac phases and whether the ratios were close to the Golden Ratio. Their results indicate that the diastolic to systolic time interval ratio is 1.611 and the RR/diastolic ratio is 1.618. They conclude that our hearts beat in a ratio of 1.618, which "obeys the beautiful order of universe settled by God" and "that our souls reside in our hearts", which, it could be argued, provides a more mystic or even religious outlook on their results.

Yetkin, Topbas, Yanik and Yetkin (2014) conducted further research as to whether systolic and diastolic blood pressure followed the Golden Ratio. They included 462 subjects who underwent ambulatory blood pressure monitoring retrospectively over a 24-hour period. Mean values of systolic and diastolic pressure levels were taken with daytime and night-time recordings assessed to calculate the ratios of these measurements. Only night-time systolic and diastolic blood pressure ratios of 1.64 and 1.62, respectively, were reported to indicate concordance with the Golden Ratio. Conversely, daytime measurements reported systolic and diastolic blood pressure ratios of 1.57 and 1.75, respectively. The authors did refer to potential variables as to why there is a significant difference between daytime and night-time ratios. For example, they believe increased daily activities may have enhanced cardiac output and peripheral vascular resistance, alongside a natural decrease in blood pressure from wake to sleep, which is often associated with a substantial decrease in sympathetic nerve measurements.

More recently, Yetkin, Celik, Arpaci and Ileri (2015) investigated the relationship between echocardiographic parameters and the Golden Ratio in 1,412 healthy patients. They concluded from their results that the ratio between the left ventricular end-diastolic and end-systolic diameters provided a ratio of 1.614, which is close to the Golden Ratio, therefore positing that the left ventricular diameters exactly obey Euclid's concept of the Golden Ratio. However, it is important to note that there currently remains a paucity of empirical evidence or systematic understanding of how the Golden Ratio contributes to cardiovascular structure and function. Moreover, although it is important to recognise the inquisitive nature of the above authors, an element of caution is required in relation to the literature reported by Yetkin et al. (2013, 2014, 2015). Firstly, these papers were letters to the editor of the *Journal of Cardiology* and not full scientific papers, despite the healthy sample sizes used in all studies that could have allowed for publishing in a far more extensive manner. Secondly, there are elements of the methods and analytical processes applied that are somewhat questionable, considering the claims the authors are reporting within their conclusions. It is here that the 20th-century impetus to concord with evidence-based practice approaches has to be considered. So much so, as Iosa (2016) states, in response to the authors' continued reference to the not well-defined spiritual, mystic and even religious forces that influence the cardiovascular system, a letter was sent to the journal editor to remind them of the importance of systematic references and data to substantiate these claims.

Another area of growing interest has been represented by investigations of the Golden Ratio and its relative applicability to electrocardiography (ECG) testing. During their recent study of ECG responses to submaximal exercise from the perspective of Golden Ratio harmonic rhythm, Ciucurel et al. (2018) tested a group of 230 young subjects, each performing a six-minute submaximal exercise ergometer test. What interested the authors was the estimate and ratio of difference between the electrical diastole and electrical systole, and between the cardiac cycle and electrical diastole, as this has previously been discussed as being closely linked to the value of the Golden Ratio. They proposed the use of a new synthetic fractal indicator (SFI) to determine the intervals of acceptability. Their results indicated that the mean values of the SFI were close to the value of the Golden Ratio, which suggests the presence of harmonic rhythm, under various conditions of existence and adaptation. While there have been a few research studies conducted around this topic, there have been scant empirical investigations to substantiate the claims made here. The authors also note that there was a lack of focus around assessing the parameters and variability during the data collection procedure; therefore, this could have impacted the validity and credibility of such findings.

Biomechanics and kinesiology

Other fields of musculoskeletal medicine such as human biomechanics and kinesiology have become vehicles for new paradigmatic sufficiency in relation to the Golden Ratio, especially considering that, within the perfect symmetry of 1:1, it is impossible to discern walking from running due to the integral stance and swing phases required for normal loco-motion. Increasing interest in the various phases of the gait cycle, for example by Iosa et al. (2013), has fuelled research primarily focused on the delineation of components of the swing and stance phases of gait. Iosa et al.'s research illuminated data from 20 subjects and noted that the ratio between the stance and swing phases seem to coincide with the Golden Ratio. Consistent with the extant literature to date, their research revealed that the percentage of the stride at which the foot is reliably lifted from the ground is between 60% and 62%. However, the distinct delineation from all knowledge to date, identified in this research, was an oversight of previous research: until that point, it had never been formally identified that the mean percentage of the foot lift-off was not of significant diffe-rence from 1 to the Golden Ratio, with 0.618 being expressible as 61.8%. Several caveats that may have impacted on the credibility of these claims, such as age, speed and terrain inclination, were also identified, which were not directly addressed during the study.

The concept of this "Golden Gait" has developed traction in this field of disciplinary research. Tez and Kuscu (2017) are making links to more advanced and innovative applications such as robotics; however, the general consensus among prominent researchers in this field is that further extensive research is warranted to establish and investigate the perception of the Golden Ratio and its inherent links with the human locomotor system (Iosa et al., 2018).

Art, architecture and aesthetics

The Renaissance was not only a fervent period of activity in art, philosophy, literature and culture; it was also the beginning of a period in which intellectual discovery promoted the exploration of artistic and scientific phenomena. It was at this time that perception of the Golden Ratio shifted in direction from being predominately mathematically based to being extended to the creative arts and the natural world. Although the Golden Ratio was to be found in many pieces of art prior to the Renaissance period, it was then that mathematics and the Golden Ratio became an integral part of artistic representation in providing new visual perspectives (Dominte, 2015).

Several artists during the Renaissance period played pivotal roles in the contribution to the knowledge and understanding of mathematics as a fundamentally unique epistemological discipline; however, perhaps none more so than Leonardo da Vinci. His discoveries and profound contributions to the fields of mathematics, arts and science remain timeless and at the fore of aesthetic and scientific beauty and achievement in the 21st century. Perhaps one of his most well-known masterpieces, the *Vitruvian Man* – which represents an amalgamation of his primary interests of art, science and mathematics – is the best example of the Golden Ratio R from an anthropometric perspective. It originated from the Renaissance period in which a book entitled *De Devine Proportine*, by the mathematician Pacioli, provided new insight into the Fibonacci sequence and its relationship with the Golden Ratio (Iosa et al., 2018). The artworks used to illustrate this were created by da Vinci, who used anatomically harmonic proportions based on the Golden Ratio throughout his works. Pacioli in 1509 controversially suggested that this number was *prima facie* evidence of God's existence.

The Golden Ratio has also been discussed with regard to its use in architectural and gothic cathedral constructions since the Middles Ages, with Frederik Macody Lund being one of its most famous advocates. However, while his theoretical propositions at the time were widely rejected, there has been considerable debate among scholars as to the presence of the Golden Ratio in medieval architecture. This remains a much-contested aspect of academic debate. Fehér, Szilágyi and Halmos (2018) recently attempted to address this in their report which specifically focused on the role that the Golden Ratio and Fibonacci sequence played in original pentagonal constructions by medieval architects. While they predominantly reviewed historical texts from several medieval sources such as Mathias Roriczer's *Geometrica Deutsch* and *The Musterbuch* by Hans Hammer, they primarily focused on the most commonly cited and best-known pentagonal drawing of a tower of five edges, referred to as the Portfolio of Villard de Honnecourt dating back to the 13th century. They assessed that there were several architectural examples that evidenced the importance of the pentagon in their constructions. However, it was difficult to ascertain as to whether medieval architects were consistently and knowingly applying concepts associated with the Golden Ratio and the Fibonacci sequence on each occasion. Moreover, they did conclude that the approximation of 72 degrees is likely to have been crucial for the pentagonal construction in Villard de Honnecourt's sketchbook, in conjunction with an approximation of the Golden Ratio that could have possibly been achieved from the pairs of the Fibonacci sequence.

The Golden Ratio has intrigued researchers from an aesthetic perspective since the ancient Greeks posed the question as to what is the meaning of beauty. Is it entirely a subjective matter and of arbitrary personal preference, or could there actually be some underpinning scientific principles that perhaps influence and guide our perception of beauty? According to Alam et al. (2015), the Golden Ratio has been shown to manifest itself throughout the human form, such as in the face, teeth and structural skeleton. Perhaps, seeing as the Golden Ratio seemingly has the influence to evoke aesthetically pleasing effects, could it be built into our consciousness as human beings as a method to steer our judgements? Some of the existing body of research has strived to provide an answer to these queries, with some suggesting that beautiful facial structures have anthropometric measurements that are closely aligned to the Golden Ratio (Ricketts, 1982; Pancherz, Knapp, Erbe and Heiss, 2010). Several other research studies over the past two decades have utilised different methods to analyse and assess the facial aesthetics by anthropometrical means, such as direct facial measurements, photographs and even through angular and linear analyses of soft tissue profiles, with some attempting to classify facial shapes across a range of different genders and ethnicities using the Golden Ratio to determine prevalence (Saraswathi, 2007; Naini, Donaldson, McDonald and Cobourne, 2012; Sunilkumar et al., 2013).

Conclusion

The debate as to whether the Fibonacci sequence and Golden Ratio provide a divine insight into universal design, via what is often viewed as an irrational number, continues, despite their transcendence of worldly disciplinarity. As such, their exact epistemological positioning remains a key challenge in their theoretical and conceptual positioning. As a concept, the Golden Ratio has undoubtedly captured the fascination of scholars and intellectuals since its recognition. What must be acknowledged alongside any lauding of the concept, though, is that in relation to an evidence-based presentation of it, the personal epistemological stance of researchers in the field may have been biased in their own epistemic beliefs of what the Golden Ratio constitutes. Contrastingly, some researchers have attempted to focus their attention on the mystic or even the monotheistic creator presence that the Golden Ratio has evidenced, transcending disciplinarity, and do not believe it should be subjected to the same level of scientific scrutiny by modern societies as a consequence of the potential implications of questioning God (Iosa et al., 2018).

What is clear, though, is that any discussion of the Fibonacci sequence or the Golden Ratio leads us directly back to the relevance of the epistemology of mathematics as an applied discipline. While it has been suggested that the epistemology of mathematics differs significantly from creative artistic practice and the natural sciences, with some claiming that it is disconnected from reality and its sociocultural origins and influences, it is clear these standpoints can be contested. However, the debate around the presence of the Fibonacci sequence and Golden Ratio only further illuminates the epistemic exception that mathematics is and has become. In its truest sense, mathematics can be positioned beyond disciplinarity, encapsulating the basis for human's ongoing fascination with it.

References

Abbott, D (2013). The reasonable ineffectiveness of mathematics. *Proceedings of the IEEE, 101*(10), 2147–2153.

Adam, M, Piatek, B, Pleszczynski, M, Smolen, B & Witula, R (2016). Certain inequalities connected with the Golden Ratio and the Fibonacci numbers. *Journal of Applied Mathematics and Computational Mechanics, 15*(1), 5–15.

Alam, MK, Noor, NFM, Basri, R, Yew, TF & Wen, TH (2015). Multiracial facial Golden Ratio and evaluation of facial appearance. *PLoS ONE, 10*(11), 1–22.

Ashrafian, H & Athanasiou, T (2011). Fibonacci series and coronary anatomy. *Heart Lung Circulation, 20*(7), 483–484.

Boniface, J (2007). The concept of number from Gauss to Kronecker. In C Goldstein, N Schappacher & J Schwermer (Eds). *The Shaping of Arithmetic After CF Gauss's Disquisitiones Arithmeticae* (pp.314–342). Berlin: Springer-Verlag Berlin Heidelberg.

Buldt, B, Lowe, B & Muller, T (2008). Towards a new epistemology of mathematics. *Erkenn, Open Access, 68*(3), 309–329.

Ciucurel, C, Georgescu, L & Iconaru, EI (2018). ECG response to submaximal exercise from the perspective of Golden Ratio harmonic rhythm. *Biomedical Signalling and Processing and Control, 40*, 156–160.

Clarke-Doane, J (2014). Moral epistemology: The mathematics analogy. *Nous, 48*(2), 238–255.

Dominte, C (2015). The golden section is a golden symbol. *University of Bucharest Review: Religion and Spirituality in Literature and Arts, 1*, 13–20.

Ernest, P (1995). Values, gender and images of mathematics: A philosophical perspective. *International Journal of Mathematical Education in Science and Technology, 26*(3), 449–462.

Fehér, K, Szilágyi, B & Halmos, B (2018). Golden Ratio and Fibonacci sequence in pentagonal constructions of medieval architecture. *Journal of Built Environment*, *6*(1), 37–46.

Grattan-Guinness, I (2004). The mathematics of the past: Distinguishing its history from our heritage. *Historia Mathematica*, *31*(2), 163–185.

Greco, J & Sosa, E (1999). *The Blackwell Guide to Epistemology*. Oxford: Blackwell Publishers.

Higgins, PM (1998). *Mathematics for the Curious*. Oxford: Oxford University Press.

Iosa, M (2016). Golden Ratio and the heart, God and the science. *International Journal of Cardiology*, *222*, 762–763.

Iosa, M, Morone, G, Marrchetti, F, Caltragirone, C, et al. (2013). The Golden Ratio of gait harmony: Repetitive proportions of repetitive gait phases. *Biomedical Research International*, *2013*(918642), 1–7.

Iosa, M, Morone, G & Paolucci, S (2018). Phi in physiology, psychology and biomechanics: The Golden Ratio between myth and science. *BioSystems*, *165*, 31–39.

Kant, I (1998). *Critique of Pure Reason* (trans. P Guyer & AW Wood). Cambridge: Cambridge University Press.

Lave, JW & Wenger, EE (1991). *Situated Learning: Legitimate Peripheral Participation*. Cambridge: Cambridge University Press.

Lee, HJ & Shin, K (2013). Grassmann's mathematical epistemology and generalization of vector spaces. *Journal for History of Mathematics*, *26*(4), 245–257.

Naini, FB, Donaldson, AN, McDonald, F & Cobourne, MT (2012). Assessing the influence of chin prominence on perceived attractiveness in the orthognathic patient, clinician and lay person. *International Journal Oral Maxillofacial Surgery*, *41*(7), 839–846.

Ozturk, S, Yalta, K & Yetkin, E (2016). Golden Ratio: A subtle regulator on our body and cardiovascular system? *International Journal of Cardiology*, *223*, 143–145.

Pancherz, H, Knapp, V, Erbe, C & Heiss, AM (2010). Divine proportions in attractive and nonattractive faces. *World Journal of Orthodontics*, *11*(1), 27–36.

Prediger, S (2003). Mathematics – Cultural product or epistemic exception? In *The History of the Concept of the Formal Sciences*. Papers of the conference *Foundations of the Formal Sciences IV* (pp.217–232). Bonn.

Restivo, S (2017). *Sociology, Science, and the End of Philosophy: How Society Shapes Brains, Gods, Maths, and Logics*. Cham, Switzerland: Springer Nature.

Ricketts, RM (1982). Divine proportion in facial esthetics. *Clinical Plastic Surgery*, *9*(4), 401–422.

Saraswathi, P (2007). The golden proportion and its application to the human face. *European Journal of Anatomy*, *11*(3), 177–180.

Schroeder, J (2000). Mathematik. In H Reich, A Holzbrecher & HJ Roth (Eds). Fachdidaktik interkulturell. Ein Handbuch (pp.451–468). Opladen, Germany: Leske + Budrich.

Shapiro, S (2000). *Thinking About Mathematics: The Philosophy of Mathematics*. Oxford: Oxford University Press.

Sunilkumar, LN, Jadhav, KS, Nazirkar G, Singh, S, Nagmode, PS & Ali, M (2013). Assessment of facial golden proportions among North Maharashtrian population. *International Journal of Oral Health, 5*(3), 48–54.

Tez, T & Kuscu, H (2017). Generation of gait pattern for a biped robot by using the golden gait algorithm. *International Science Conference. Unitech Proceedings, 1,* 230–236.

Yetkin, G, Celik, T, Arpaci, M & Ileri, M (2015). Left ventricular diameters as a reflection of "extreme and mean ratio". *International Journal of Cardiology, 198,* 85–86

Yetkin, G, Sivri, N, Yalta, K & Yetkin, E (2013). Golden Ratio is beating in our heart. *International Journal of Cardiology, 168*(5), 4926–4927.

Yetkin, G, Topbas, U, Yanik, A & Yetkin, G (2014). Does systolic and diastolic blood pressure follow Golden Ratio? *International Journal of Cardiology, 176*(3), 1457–1459.

3

ILLUSTRATING THE TRANSCENDENCE OF DISCIPLINARITY

Catherine Hayes, Claire Todd and Stephen Capper

> *Knowledge has three degrees – opinion, science, and illumination. The means or instrument of the first is sense; of the second, dialectic; of the third, intuition. This last is absolute knowledge founded on the identity of the mind knowing with the object known.*
>
> Plotinus (204 CE–274 CE)

Introduction

This chapter illustrates where the transcendence of disciplinarity in philosophical and epistemological thinking is being used in applied practice, and we have chosen human anatomy to illuminate perspectives in this field. Examples of this include the use of cadavers in artistic practice and the use of somaesthetics in science. The focus is on the central debate of whether anything can actually be categorised as purely art or purely science in terms of disciplinarity. We engage with the concept of how we can measure the physiological impact of art, and we consider the wealth of historical artefacts which have been used as a fundamental basis for the development of innovative new methodological approaches in practice-based research. Gross anatomical structure has been the focus of art and science since the Renaissance, where the epistemological basis of life itself was a core focus of curiosity, wonderment and inaccessibility for most. The relational capacity we have to align, compare and integrate the notions of functionalism and aesthetics is demonstrated in this context and, perhaps more than anywhere else, in applied onto-epistemology.

Deviation from the normal had become a spectacle by the early 19th century with the emergence of "freak shows", where disease and deformity were used for entertainment purposes while simultaneously denigrating those living with long-term medical and genetic conditions. While human anatomy can undoubtedly educate, entertain and provide a conduit between art and science, it also provides a raft of opportunities to reconnect and engage people in considering the notion of mortality, longevity and the inevitability of death; and it holds the basis for the opportunity of holism and existentialism at its metaphorical heart.

The interrelationship of meaning-making and interpretation

To consider the transcendence of disciplinarity in practice in both art and medicine, it is useful to examine the notion that the relationship between meaning-making and interpretation is also significant (Adkins, 2019). This relationship is an embodied legacy of the earliest emergence of public dissection displays in 3000 BCE, when anatomical theatre was first documented (Bauch, 2017). Aligned with this is the documentation of the original historical power balances between art and anatomy in practice (Brown, 2017). Western anatomy was not institutionalised in Europe until the mid-16th century, with the exception of Italy where human dissection had featured in medical curricula as early as 1286, and where it had become an embedded part of all Italian medical curricula by the mid-14th century (Di Marco, 2015). Italian and Dutch dissection facilitated the first interdisciplinary praxis between anatomy and artistry, most significantly in Bologna, Padua and Leiden, where the longevity of human anatomy exhibitions and representations still pervades modern exhibition space as a testimony of the origins of the relationship between two synergistic academic and creative disciplines (Di Marco, 2015).

The Renaissance and Baroque alliance of artistry and anatomy pervades historical artefacts that bear testimony to the power balance between the two (Kemp, 2010; Fulford, Lee and Kitson, 2004). Whereas the finely tuned psychomotor skill and precise underpinning cognitive knowledge of anatomists were acknowledged as intellectually prestigious, artistry was regarded as a subservient discipline where its skilful practitioners unwittingly became the first medical illustrators, capturing the internal viscera of human subjects in the form of the first intricate anatomical plates (Proctor, 1991). The reframing of this relationship is illuminated most significantly in the context of contemporary art. The tradition of reliance of an artist on the anatomist has disappeared with the emergence of preserved specimens and relatively open access to anatomical specimens in practice (Gillispie, 2016; Lantos, 2011; Casini, 2011).

Historical and philosophical thinking: Exhibits of art and social science

The trajectory of knowledge and its presentation to society and in differing cultural settings is illustrated well by anatomy and artistry. In recent years, the shift in onto- epistemological ownership of medical anatomy and, subsequently, artistry that Gunther von Hagens unveiled was facilitated by his revolutionary preserving technique of plastination (Scott, 2008; von Hagens, Whalley, Kunkel and Kelly, 2000). Not without controversy, his Body Worlds exhibitions freely and openly extended the relationship and interdependency between objectification and visualisation that exist between art and anatomy from a historical and philosophical perspective (Katz, 2017; Kirk, 2009; Moore and Brown, 2007). The process of plastination has ensured that educational anatomy and artistry are equal partners in the public exhibition of human viscera, which have been brought to the wholesale accessibility of the public masses (Swanson, Newman, Araque and Dubinsky, 2017). Ironically, one of the most famous examples of tacit knowledge is the concept of facial recognition. Tacit knowledge enables us to recognise a face among millions of others (Polanyi, 1967); yet the stark anonymity that surface skin removal ensures, in the context of von Hagens' anatomical artistry, also provides a means of discerning what is knowable, what is recognisable and what is an innate part of the human psyche (Stone, 2011). This academic debate is extended further in a consideration of where the capacity for reflection and critical reflexivity exists as an embodiment of experience and intrinsic engagement (Archibald, Caine and Scott, 2017; Burns, 2007; Kinsella, 2007).

While the cross-cutting theme of transcending disciplines in human anatomy is clear cut, other disciplines also feature heavily in the consideration of the human body, its origins, its beauty and its ownership (Bairaktarova, 2017; Toom, 2012). From this perspective, it is important to consider what von Hagens himself has termed the "democratisation of anatomy", where the issue of accessibility to dissected cadavers is posited as a means of sanitising and removing the power that had made human anatomical dissection a shrouded secret from the masses since Renaissance times (Jones and Whitaker, 2009). Ironically, the enforced posture of corpses or cadavers (known in this context as "plastinates") has determined a resurrection of the dead from a dissection table to the portrayal of life personified by a faceless and anonymised community, to whom the public immediately relate – partially due to the characteristic "sameness" of faces with skin removed (Polanyi, 1967). Context and presentation are everything, and the drama of lighting and glass casing ensures the accessibility of an exhibit and a level of sanitation and protection far removed from the smell of formaldehyde and the glimmer of the anatomist's scalpel (Jones and Whitaker, 2009).

Perhaps the greatest example of Renaissance artistry is evident in the depiction of Michelangelo's St Bartholomew from the Sistine Chapel (1508–1512), an image replicated too in the work of von Hagens' male model, who also holds his entire skin aloft. He holds his entire skin in his upheld hand, thus facially anonymised and creating "a sense of community among all humankind" (Moore and Brown, 2007) and, through this, somehow justifying the use of plastination as the historical legacy of anatomists and their discipline-specific artistry. In humanising life through death, what von Hagens achieves is not just the transcendence of disciplinarity, but the embodiment of human transcendence from the here and now to the eternal, with a blatant celebration of how physicality underlines all possible human achievement. As such, this compels the observer to contemplate their identity in the transience of life, its purpose, its meaning and the futility of rationalistic health education (Moore and Brown, 2007).

Such is the level of functional psychomotor skill necessary for the exquisite dissection work represented in Body Worlds that it is unsurprising that many anatomists are unfamiliar with the deep theological and enlightening nature of their work (Jones and Whitaker, 2009). While anatomy remains a biological scientific discipline, its capacity to define both tacit and rational tangible knowledge is arguably unsurpassed in relation to just how many disciplines it can transcend.

Technology and the emergence of the World Wide Web in the 20th century has assured that what was traditionally regarded as morally and ethically unacceptable is now accessible to all who wish to satisfy their curiosity about death as the ultimate culmination of a life lived.

The contextual and situational nature of knowledge documented by Toom (2012) highlights the relative complexity of both philosophy and psychology. Where von Hagens excels is in his ability to provide complexity and ambiguity in artistic representation with which people can relate to and be educated by. His tacit knowledge dimensionality transcends both what is tangible and what remains universally unknown to all those still alive. Toom describes tacit knowledge as an "accumulated product of thinking and action, and also as a process during action". With von Hagens, this is reconciled with a consideration of how rational it is to place emphasis on public health in the face of the inevitable outcome of death. His work may highlight human shortfalls in bodily maintenance, but a certain irony pervades when we contemplate the fact that, however hard humans try, they are still destined for a worldly exit in a predictably and relatively short time frame. It is also here that Toom observes the common themes that characterise a human's perception of a tangible world with the gaze of a mere mortal.

Debating the transcendence of disciplinarity in art and science

During both the 19th and 20th centuries, the crude and blatant categorisation of whether academic disciplines and their professional praxes were either "science" or "art" typified themes of scholarly debate. This coincided temporally with the rise of modernism as a new form of knowledge, the industrialisation of nations and the debate around whether art and science should have distinguishable goals. As a consequence, the rise in modernism led to practitioners from both creative practice and science to contrast and polarise their specific domains, which saw territorial protection of knowledge as "belonging" to either one or the other, rather than being a shared intellectual endeavour (Jones and Galison, 1998). Apparent at that time was the notion that both domains of practice had shaped a definition of their own intellectual practice, and that art occupied the role of the creative mind and was perceived as the preservation of tradition and conservation of human values. In contrast, science became perceived as something that suppressed spontaneity and creative impulse and advocated a purist scientific lens for knowledge that was inextricably linked with industrial processes and the evolution of technology (Wilson, 2010; Jones and Galison, 1998). It is debatable that, perhaps, this was due to the lack of consensus regarding an operational definition of each. According to Wilson (2010), science is often viewed as the measurement of natural phenomena through the utilisation of traditional scientific methods of inquiry, such as the formulation of hypotheses, experiments or observations to test and then draw conclusions from. In contrast, Strosberg (2001) states that the term science embodies studies that carry a universal meaning that can be irrefutably proven by rigorous research methodologies on the basis of verifiable facts, which provide knowledge of the inhabited world. The nature of truth though, stemming from the ontological basis of this debate, ensures that the epistemology underpinning it means that a purist operational definition of what art is or has the potential to be is virtually impossible. This has been a feature of philosophical debate for centuries.

Continuing on from the Renaissance, temporality became a classic feature of the capacity of researchers to position epistemological stance in relation to rationalism and empiricism. Creative practice and its epistemological basis, as a direct consequence of this, have alluded to the need or possibility for definition. Historically, this was regularly pondered by philosophers such as Plato (429–347 BCE) and Aristotle (384–322 BCE), who focused the need for epistemological understanding on such creative practices as poetry and the composition of dramatic and epic performances, alongside traditional dance and musicology. Painting and sculpture were the preserve of the elite and were predominantly regarded as being for aesthetic purpose via the creation of exploratory symbols and beauty. It is also notable that until the 16th century, neither were justified conceptually or theoretically in literature (Ribeiro, 2015).

Perceived reality lies at the heart of being able to distinguish between and delineate the epistemological bases of art and science; yet, in reality, they are often exactly the same. For example, how are acrobatic performances perceived? Do they dangerously teeter between mechanical concepts based on co-ordination, balance and agility, or a finely tuned artistic performance rooted epistemologically in creative practice (Stafford, 1999)?

One of the key debates surrounding the work of Gunther von Hagens is not his usage of plastinates to represent and demonstrate the functional reality of human anatomy in the context of public dissections, but whether he can be defined as a skilled anatomist or a skilled creative practitioner, rooted in the notion of performativity and sensationalism characterised by his capacity for artistry in public fora (Stephens, 2011). Young (2001) advocates that art and science are both powerful sources of and contributors to knowledge, but that their worldly representation is multidimensional. Science has often been posited as the ultimate method of systematic inquiry, yet the capacity to embed discernment and tacit knowledge arguably stems from art and creative practice, whose inquisitive methods are often grounded in observation. Whereas empirical scientists may use experimentation as a mechanism of developing knowledge prior to the construction of new knowledge or theory, the arts of contemplation and observation adopted by artists provide a human lens for interpretation, which acknowledges the authentic and actively facilitates meaning-making.

According to Calne (1996), the predilection of artists in the Renaissance period for conducting research studies on the human body to ascertain its physiological function and anatomical structure, prior to representing the body, was influenced by a shift in perspective to realism.

In this context, visual images could be used for the two distinct, yet irrefutably interconnected, purposes of communicating pertinent information or of contributing to aesthetics.

Across all disciplinary boundaries, it is arguable that the most famous Renaissance figure was Leonardo da Vinci (1452–1519). Not only was he a painter, sculptor, architect and inventor, da Vinci excelled in transcending academic disciplines through his liberation of medicine and art from restrictions of previous regimes imposed upon both disciplines by society and the Church. His work also transcends the concept of temporality, with Kirby (2017), a renowned podiatric medic, stating that da Vinci's description of the human foot, as a "masterpiece of engineering and a work of art", encapsulates the complexities from a biomechanical perspective, yet also depicts the natural beauty of the foot. Globally, podiatrists, orthopaedic surgeons and human engineers still marvel at the mechanical science of the foot during both weight-bearing and non-weight-bearing activity. Da Vinci's notebooks and sketchbooks remain a source of illumination to them to this day.

While art and science are often indisputably epistemologically connected, the manner in which each contributes and actively represents knowledge often remains distinct from the other. Ede (2005) argues that today's society is better informed on contemporary science as opposed to contemporary art; perhaps this is due to technological advancements or how these are perceived in the modern media. This debate is then extended into the suggestion that people are more likely to subscribe to reported facts and empirical evidence supported by the scientific method, as this is regarded as a gold standard in a society driven by the need for a quantifiable evidence base.

Pivotal to the delineation of the epistemology of both art and science is the notion of paradigmatic sufficiency. Paradigms from Kuhn's (1970) perspectives were a formulation of how bodies of knowledge could be subjected to classification and methodological deconstruction. Typically, scientific knowledge such as anatomy was classified as a medical discipline in relation to the context of medical research. Its contested or complementary position in art, however, reveals an idiosyncratic contribution to the aesthetic beauty of nature, so often represented by art in the context of creative practice. Another key consideration, as highlighted by Hothersall (2019), is the notion of the pragmatic application of knowledge and whether this is positioned theoretically, or directly applied, in pragmatic terms. Within the context of human interpretation, this work highlighted the need for recognition that knowledge can never be absolute, because it is characterised by the capacity for situational change of context/temporality and perception by others. Also significant are the "rationale for knowing" and the "nature of justification".

In relation to this, Power (2015) considers the debate around positivist epistemological approaches with scientific evidence at the forefront of what is generally considered "gold standard" information, but which fails to acknowledge the integration of tacit knowledge in practice, and how this irrefutably impacts the capacity for clinical decision-making by medical practitioners. It is the constructivist paradigm which places emphasis on the situated nature of knowledge and its temporality, so that tacit knowledge and intuitive reasoning are integral to and an authentic part of enhanced clinical decision-making. Gobbi (2005) reinforces this stance, highlighting intuitive practice as an artistic and mythical concept characterised by the indefinable and irrational. In contrast though, Hajjaj, Salek, Basra and Finlay (2010) suggest that it is merely a by-product of experiential knowledge and expertise, and is therefore just an adjunct to an evidence base rooted in cognate disciplines. Obstetrics and gynaecology is arguably one of the best disciplines to demonstrate where both positivist and constructivist approaches are combined in the context of cognitive integration, with intuitive thinking via tacit knowledge construction in clinical practice (Jackson, Hayes and Hinshaw, 2013; Power, 2015; Thornton, 2006).

Conclusion

It is arguable that art and science are perhaps bound most by human fascination of their differences which, ironically, allows them to reveal the need for the creation of new knowledge that encompasses and acknowledges the inherent value of each to a knowledge society. Ede (2005) warns of the chaos and uncertainty that attempts to combine the two can bring, and it is perhaps here that they need to allow one to complement the other in the context of innovative scientific discovery and intellectual endeavour. The former would not be possible without key artistic concepts such as visualisation, daydreaming, storytelling and abstracting. In contrast, Wilson (2010) believes art and science to be the driving engines behind creativity in modern society, and the compartmentalisation of these methods of inquiry would result in a distinct lack of capacity to transcend disciplinarity and collaborative effort.

References

Adkins, J (2019). Authenticity in anatomy art. *Journal of Medical Humanities*, 40(1), 117–138.

Archibald, MM, Caine, V & Scott, SD (2017). Intersections of the arts and nursing knowledge. *Nursing Inquiry*, 24(2), E12153.

Bairaktarova, D (2017). The new Renaissance artificers: Harnessing the power of creativity in the engineering classroom. In D Bairaktarova & M Eodice (Eds). *Creative Ways of Knowing in Engineering* (pp.1–22). Cham, Switzerland: Springer International Publishing.

Bauch, N (2017). Practicing spatial epistemology with Immanuel Kant's "physical" classification. *International Journal of Humanities and Arts Computing, 11*(1), 55–67.

Brown, NC (2017). Art education curriculum praxis: A time for collaboration. In NCM Brown (Ed.). *Studies in Philosophical Realism in Art, Design and Education* (pp.79–93). Cham, Switzerland: Springer International Publishing.

Burns, L (2007). Gunther von Hagens' Body Worlds: Selling beautiful education. *The American Journal of Bioethics, 7*(4), 12–23.

Calne, R (1996). *Art Surgery and Transplantation.* London: Williams & Williams.

Casini, S (2011). Magnetic resonance imaging (MRI) as mirror and portrait: MRI configurations between science and the arts. *Configurations, 19*(1), 73–99.

Di Marco, S (2015). Bodies of knowledge: Anatomy and transparency in contemporary art. *Journal of Science and Technology of the Arts, 7*(2), 33.

Ede, S (2005). *Art and Science.* London: IB Tauris.

Fulford, T, Lee, D & Kitson, PJ (2004). *Literature, Science and Exploration in the Romantic Era: Bodies of Knowledge* (Vol. 60). Cambridge: Cambridge University Press.

Gillispie, CC (2016). *The Edge of Objectivity: An Essay on the History of Scientific Ideas.* Princeton, NJ: Princeton University Press.

Gobbi M (2005). Nursing practice as bricoleur activity: A concept explored. *Nursing Inquiry, 12*(2), 117–125.

Hajjaj FM, Salek, MS, Basra, MKA & Finlay, AY (2010). *Non-clinical influences on clinical decision-making: A major challenge to evidence-based practice. Journal of Royal Society of Medicine, 103*(5), 178–187.

Hothersall, SJ (2019). Epistemology and social work: Enhancing the integration of theory, practice and research through philosophical pragmatism. *European Journal of Social Work, 22*(5), 860–870.

Jackson, KS, Hayes, K & Hinshaw, K (2013). The relevance of non-technical skills in obstetrics and gynaecology. *The Obstetrician & Gynaecologist, 15*(4), 269–274.

Jones, CA & Galison, P (Eds) (1998). *Picturing Science, Producing Art.* Basingstoke, UK: Routledge.

Jones, DG & Whitaker, MI (2009). Engaging with plastination and the Body Worlds phenomenon: A cultural and intellectual challenge for anatomists. *Clinical Anatomy, 22*(6), 770–776.

Katz, P (2017). Introduction: Drawing and science are inseparable. In P Katz (Ed.). *Drawing for Science Education: An International Perspective* (pp.1–8). Rotterdam, The Netherlands: Sense Publishers.

Kemp, M (2010). Style and non-style in anatomical illustration: From Renaissance Humanism to Henry Gray. *Journal of Anatomy, 216*(2), 192–208.

Kinsella, EA (2007). Embodied reflection and the epistemology of reflective practice. *Journal of Philosophy of Education, 41*(3), 395–409.

Kirby, K (2017). Longitudinal arch loading-sharing system of the foot. *Revisita Espanola de Podologia, 28*(1), 18–26.

Kirk, F (2009). *Grotesque Inscriptions: Liberal Optics and Spectacles of the Dead.* East Lansing, MI: Michigan State University.

Kuhn, TS (1970). *The Structure of Scientific Revolutions* (Unabridged, 2nd ed.). Chicago: University of Chicago Press.

Lantos, JD (Ed.) (2011). *Controversial Bodies: Thoughts on the Public Display of Plastinated Corpses.* Baltimore, MD: JHU Press.

Moore, CM & Brown, CM (2007). Experiencing Body Worlds: Voyeurism, education, or enlightenment? *Journal of Medical Humanities, 28*(4), 231–254.

Polanyi, M (1967). Sense-giving and sense-reading. *Philosophy, 42*(162), 301–325.

Power, A (2015). Contemporary midwifery practice: Art, science or both? *British Journal of Midwifery, 23*(9), 654–657.

Proctor, R (1991). *Value-free Science? Purity and Power in Modern Knowledge.* Cambridge, MA: Harvard University Press.

Ribeiro, AC (2015). *The Bloomsbury Companion to Aesthetics.* London: Bloomsbury.

Scott, R (2008). Anatomy of spectatorship: Tracing the body in Body Worlds, the anatomical exhibition of real human bodies. Doctoral dissertation, School of Communication, Simon Fraser University.

Stafford, MB (1999). *Artful Science: Enlightenment, Entertainment and the Eclipse of Visual Education.* London: MIT Press.

Stephens, E (2011). *Anatomy as Spectacle: Public Exhibitions of the Body from 1700 to the Present.* Liverpool: Liverpool University Press.

Stone, PR (2011). Dark tourism and the cadaveric carnival: Mediating life and death narratives at Gunther von Hagens' Body Worlds. *Current Issues in Tourism, 14*(7), 685–701.

Strosberg, E (2001). *Art and Science.* New York: Abbeville Press Publishers.

Swanson, LW, Newman, E, Araque, A & Dubinsky, JM (2017). *The Beautiful Brain: The Drawings of Santiago Ramon y Cajal.* New York: Abrams.

Thornton T (2006). Tacit knowledge as the unifying factor in evidence-based medicine and clinical judgement. *Philosophy, Ethics, Humanities and Medicine, 1*(1), E2.

Toom, A (2012). Considering the artistry and epistemology of tacit knowledge and knowing. *Educational Theory, 62*(6), 621–640.

von Hagens, G, Whalley, A, Kunkel, A & Kelly, F (2000). *Anatomy Art: Fascination Beneath the Surface.* Heidelberg: Institute for Plastination.

Wilson, S (2010). *Art and Science: How Scientific Research and Technological Innovation are Becoming Key to 21st-Century Aesthetics.* London: Thames & Hudson.

Young, YO (2001). *Art and Knowledge.* London: Routledge.

4

POSITIONALITY, KNOWLEDGE AND TRUTH

So where lies reality?

Catherine Hayes

> *Truth in philosophy means that concept and external reality correspond.*
> (Hegel, 1896)

Introduction

Positionality, knowledge and truth are all independently and ultimately determined by the situated nature of their reality. Nowhere is this of greater significance than in the establishment of what that reality is, which developing researchers often find challenging to clearly articulate and operationally define.

Historical perspectives of truth

The metaphysical basis of truth posited by key thinkers of the Middle Ages bears minimal resemblance to the preoccupation with evidence-based research approaches adopted by the vast majority of 21st-century professions in western societies. Whether "truth" can ever actually be known or established by humans at all was a fundamental and much contested debate originating from ancient philosophers and largely continued by medieval thinkers. The nature of truth and the debates surrounding it are ones which still ultimately influence our approaches to the establishment of ontological and epistemological positionality today, both for ourselves and the research questions and statements we posit. These debates often hinge around semantic meanings, but ultimately have become responsible for the fractured and delineated "ways of knowing" that characterise and shape practice in contemporaneous research across now disparate signature pedagogies and academic disciplines. Once aligned for hundreds of years, without the need for delineation at an epistemological level, the disconnect that originated from medieval thinkers has largely framed later thinking until now. Contemporaneous research reflects a systematisation and structure based on the taxonomic approaches to evidence-based practice that is still evident in applied praxis today.

The influence of religion and faith in ontology and epistemology

It is at an ontological rather than an epistemological level, though, that truth is of greatest significance in terms of its perception. It is useful, first, to contextualise and frame perspectives in faith and religiosity during the course of any academic consideration of truth and reality, as belief plays such a fundamental role in both. Medievalists advocated that the concept of truth transcended everything. Today, we speak of how the situated nature of knowledge, context specificity and temporality are fundamental to our understanding of "what is"; however, this originated from the notion that, for transcendentalists, truth is convertible "with being" (Tallant, 2017: 45–46). The Renaissance granted religion and philosophy limited credence, but its trajectory from Italy across Europe ensured its evident impact on a diverse array of disciplines including science and art, and, perhaps most importantly, on the notion of human thought and consciousness, which is still apparent today. The pragmatism it proceeded with ensured its relevance to the improvement of human existence and the capacity of scholarship to shape and orchestrate human endeavour outside of the scope of historical and religiously based superstition. This humanistic perspective engaged a paradigm shift that had held Europe to intellectual ransom for centuries. As a consequence of this, the overall aim of an education was aligned with the vision of all a human could actually be, incorporating the aesthetic as well as cognate disciplines and reconciling concepts of humanist scholarship. This impacted widely on the positionality of the Church, whose symbolic practices and rituals stemmed back to the origins of Christian worship. In fundamentally casting aside ritualistic practice that underpinned the original universal Catholic faith, the path for the Reformation was laid and the potential for change set across European communities of scholarship. As a consequence of this, accessibility to literature changed – the more people read, the more educated they became and, unsurprisingly, the more the conceptual basis of humanism was perpetuated. As an integral part of this education, there was a raft of new and innovative approaches in creative practice, which uniquely contributed to the development of novel, tacit and aesthetic knowledge, particularly in relation to music, painting and sculptural techniques.

The sciences were also impacted heavily upon by this systemic change in European intellectual infrastructure, and the Renaissance contributed irrevocably to the prevailing approach to science that actively encouraged rationality and an evidenced-based approach to belief. Indeed, it was these changes that contributed to the progression of human civilisation and remain reflected in the societies we occupy as the human race of the 21st century.

Despite its altruistic contributions to societal development and progress, though, the Renaissance also provided the European trajectory to war, with the development of navigational devices which initiated the competition for colonisation and ruthless discovery. This fuelled horrific warmongering and death for millions, but is often overlooked in the context of aesthetic Renaissance beauty.

The monarchy flourished in the situated context of the Renaissance, with the authority of the Church banished to a secondary position and as demand for political stability resonated across Europe. This resonant monarchical approach to legislative power emanated from allegiance to kingship, advocacy of the need for human inquiry and, subsequently, the full impact of the Reformation.

The rise of evidentialism

Evidentialism has become the hallmark of contemporary society, where beliefs that people possess are expected to constructively align with the evidence available to support them. Underpinning their assumptions and presuppositions about particular issues, many of which are steeped in the situated nature and sociocultural context of their lives, is often a faith that is posited as transcending the knowable. It is here that rationalising faith or positioning contemporary epistemology is fundamentally challenged. A term significant to both religious and secular life is justification – something which the Reformation fundamentally changed as the human psyche shifted to the need to empirically prove beyond doubt the validity and reliability of knowledge. It is here that the epistemic nature of believing is called into question – whether a fundamentally unchallenged belief can be posited as knowledge lies at the heart of debate in religious epistemology.

The term postmodernism as a characteristic and consequential response to the Enlightenment also frames how postmodern epistemology moves research assumptions based in the context of the real world, as opposed to controlled settings, towards the notion of relativism.

The shift from faith to logic

Logic superseded all else in medieval educational curricula; indeed, it was here that the ancestors of validity and reliability first appeared as ancient grandparents in the family tree of knowledge. How these principles have evolved to date, though, has been largely dependent on the human drive to frame scientific knowledge into systematic paradigms of thought, where scientific knowledge can thrive. Ultimately, it is the contingency of truth that matters most in shaping systematic inquiry. The evolution of epistemology was framed most evidently by medieval thinkers as they added the requisite that "true" research has to be known to be "certain" or "absolute". At this point in history the capture of truth was an epistemic goal of research. It was Ockham who stripped back and made visible sense of the hugely complicated 13th-century infrastructure that had been built to shroud and contain, to a certain extent, what epistemology actually was and had the potential to be. Truth was presented by Ockham as something defined by a predominantly scientific paradigm, characterised by logic with a degree of systematisation that made evidence intellectually tangible.

With the introduction of supposition, which had no origin or basis in ancient philosophy, medieval philosophers significantly moved the consideration of perception forward to the point where it was acknowledged that a personal assumption or presupposition "represented" whatever it signified. Gleiser's (2014) affirmation that "as the island of our knowledge grows, so do the shores of our ignorance" rings true for those who seek to challenge long-held presuppositions and assumptions about the context of workplace organisations, their cultures and contexts.

Historical perspectives in knowledge and the establishment of truth in research-based, academic and creative practices are all subtly different. The usefulness or purposefulness of research inquiry is what is of fundamental importance to the truth underpinning knowledge from these contexts. For professional doctorate students deliberating what is the rationale or motivation for their research, the question of being able to ascertain truth stems from the question of whether that truth is purely pragmatic or whether it is an epistemic means of consolidating both beliefs and assumptions.

The aim of establishing truth is therefore twofold. The value of truth is rooted in the value of having a true belief and the devaluing of having beliefs that are false. In relation to research-based practice, it is therefore possible to be forgiving of the stance and to say that epistemically rational belief simply aims to establish the truth of a situation or context.

As a broad rule, people don't believe things because they have set out to believe them; there is generally a source of tangible evidence to support their assumptions or presuppositions. Therefore, it can be posited that people have an aim of believing by being epistemically rational (as though they chose their beliefs with the aim of believing truths and ostracising falsehood from any fundamental degree of relevance). The danger amidst this approach is that if researchers begin research without first challenging their assumptions – and if they believe what they believe solely to believe in the pursuit of it – then the fundamental relationship between know-ledge, truth and belief is blatantly apparent. The aim of truth in this context ought to be to guide belief by the evidence available on any given issue or stance. What may rightly or wrongly be regarded as evidence, then, is an issue for consideration. Being sure that the aim of truth is not empty may well necessitate further empirical or interpretive investigation and, hence, mechanisms of acquiring true beliefs by seeking out further evidence. When organisations bear the cost of research to investigate core concepts of truth about themselves, then this raises issues of potential partisanship. This means organisations are funding research which, as a consequence, is not fully independent of them, and the likelihood of seeking affirmation of belief rather than truth often has to be the basis of assumption about everyday life. Considering things from an epistemic perspective, there-fore, does not guarantee or allude to any degree of truth other than the perceived realities of individuals. If self-belief is the source of guidance in the establishment of truth, then epistemically, it can be posited that ways of framing belief are nullified in terms of their generalisable or transferable value, since they are couched in the aim of truth being belief alone.

The individuality of mind is central to the concept of epistemology. Propositions stem from the constructions of people, for whom research into a specific area or discipline is a motivating factor. The ability to critically appraise and evaluate claims of truth are the very hallmarks of 21st-century research synthesis, and these are echoed by Descartes' (1641) discussion of the clarity of truth in original debates of the legitimacy of metaphysics. This was extended into current practice by Leibniz, whose theory of truth formed the basis of modern systematic inquiry.

The concept of truth

Truth is not absolute; it is built on perspectives, and it is these perspectives that form the basis of how the knowledge that researchers produce is represented, and how accessible it is to the articulation of what it actually is. Philosophically speaking, Locke's is the most aligned theoretical stance or perspective on what constitutes practice-based research: he posited that any understanding of work must emanate from experience of it.

The art of representation

Our mental and linguistic representation of knowledge is what encapsulates truth in practice. Ultimately, though, knowledge is dependent on understanding. Understanding is as much to do with the representative's audience as it is to do with the representation of knowledge and, ultimately, is something over which we, as researchers, have little control. Judgement is the crux of being able to delineate and interrogate knowledge in order to make informed decisions, therefore the complexity of moving from representation to understanding is ambiguous to say the least. It is this ambiguity and move from binary decision-making, though, that enables us to discern the difference between true intellectual capacity and base, crude engagement with raw facts. The relative gap between the two is infinite, and the need to utilise systematic inquiry as an infrastructure of support for logical thinking can be attributed to a millennia of evolutionary thinking, rather than being allocated to a single era in history. The quality of the conceptual basis of research is the foundation of all else stemming from it. Alluding to any given research idea is simply not sufficient to warrant its theoretical justification and it is this, which developing researchers must conceptually master through the alignment of their positionality, knowledge and lived truth, which in turn must also be contextualised both within themselves and the situations and contexts within which the work is executed, if either individual or collective meaning (perceived reality) is to be extrapolated from them. Propositional knowledge, as opposed to purist predication, is the vehicle driving human inquiry in the 21st century that necessitates first the rationality of any given idea.

Since the emergence of a digital society, the philosophical undertones of our approaches to scientific research have been similarly moved from the celebration of ambiguity in research inquiry towards a preference for binary, algorithmic and systematic thinking. The more celebrated reasoning has become, the less processes of intuition have been valued in the context of philosophical thought. It is this semantic paradox that has leaned human inquiry closer towards the further systematisation of capturing lived experiences and meaning. It is here that the notion of self-attributed truth and wider research perspectives, such as context and culture, have greatest resonance.

Experience and practice

In reconnecting epistemologies across disciplinary boundaries, it is pragmatism that has served the arena of systematic inquiry best in positioning reasoning in the bifold context of experience and practice. At the heart of pragmatism is an account of what it is to fully understand a posited concept.

Pragmatists posit philosophical underpinnings of the field to be exactly that – as far from notional as possible, with a degree of tangibility that still permits truth to be all encompassing, regardless of situation or context. Pragmatism in the 21st century has become a buzzword for the modernisation and renovation of science, religion, politics and education, and has arguably become a bypass for purist approaches to learning in the quest for instantaneous understanding. There is a temporal consequence of this, which gives pragmatism a transience in terms of impact that has been metaphorically alluded to by seminal authors such as Charles Sanders Peirce, but which is often underacknowledged in contemporaneous pragmatist research. The heart and soul of pragmatism is human and, as a consequence, it is inherently subjective both in its underpinning rationality and the motivation for its execution. It is the celebrated capacity for critical reflection and consequent reflexivity which provides an impetus to integrate it into several aspects of organisational managerialism, such as the management of change, quality, culture and organisational structures. The longevity of the success of pragmatism is often temporally dependent upon overarching macro-level issues of the economy, changes in politics and the geopolitical climates that frame global societies.

If we necessitate full accounts of truth, then these must be positioned in practical endeavour; it is fundamental to human thought and does not exist in abstraction from it, providing an ideal base for research-based praxis and experiential learning. It ought also to be a precursor to the recognition that researcher positionality and the articulation of it are imperative to the trustworthiness and authenticity of insider research, where researchers are often middle managers who have already made a sustained contribution to professional practice over a considerable time period in their career trajectories. Suspending presupposition is often not an issue in these situations and, therefore, an account of researcher positionality is imperative to the transparency of data interpretation from contexts of applied professional practice. Dispositional accounts of rationality ought not to detract from the broader perspective of experience in often limited settings and organisational hierarchies; although what is overlooked is often the potential for the transferability rather than generalisability of research findings from professional practice. Both authentic assertion and belief necessitate inquiry and rationality as the fundamental basis of truth in pragmatism.

Life's epiphanies and critical incidents can often be the source of challenge to long-held beliefs and assumptions. It is these which often give rise to the metaphorical portrayal of what pragmatic research actually is. Truth itself is an epistemic notion, embedded and entrenched in the meaning that researchers make of their own personal and professional experiences. It is here that the significant acknowledgement that research-based practice alludes to as approximating the truth is imperative – since all truth from the perspective of individual interpretation and understanding is relative, then truth cannot be absolute and ought to be recognised as such. This perhaps best illustrates the difference between professional doctorate research and that undertaken for a Doctorate of Philosophy. Whereas the latter is rooted in philosophical underpinning and nationality, in contrast, professional doctorate learning pathways afford candidates the opportunity to undertake first-order inquiry with a practical relevance to everyday reality and application to practice. Here, it is possible to posit that truth in this sense is something that satisfies the researcher's aims in the assertion of inquiry and, also in this sense, we can see why providing operationally definitive terms for meaning in the context of research praxis can feel so challenging in the initial phases of research.

Critical introspection as a source of implicit knowledge and truth

The motivation and rationale for practice-based research in the workplace that characterise professional doctorate programmes is often a legacy of long-held presuppositions and assumptions about the individual realities of employees. Processes of critical reflexivity and introspection have become the mechanisms by which these can be actively deconstructed and effectively challenged and understood, which consequently paves the way for systematic inquiry as opposed to cheerleading a specific cause or grinding an anecdotal axe. These processes are an integral part of the mid-career professional's opportunities to build and develop professional identity at a much deeper level, and they provide an insight into how best new ways of thinking and approaching what is perceived can illuminate truth, as opposed to simply a perceived reality. The notion of participative scoping and learning is central to being able to challenge these often long-held presuppositions; and the degree of performativity that underpins the process of critical introspection is fundamentally important in justifying its worth. In reporting an insight into professional identity, it is imperative to remember that this does not constitute an epistemic insight, but that any constructivist perspective on the depiction of reality ought to underpin the professional with the personal. Such a discursive approach hinges on the capacity to compartmentalise and prioritise a life lived and to extract the fundamental relevance of it to research-based practice. Throughout a career trajectory, it is possible to construct and articulate a progressive identity – identity is temporal, dynamic and, in relation to lived experience, is never actually complete or fully tangible (Ellis, 1991).

The epistemological basis of identity building is therefore a means of articulating a series of relatively minor epiphanies or small transformative learning experiences, which cumulatively shape an epistemic sense of being. It is here that the dichotomy between individual epistemic introspection and disciplinary based reflexivity merges. Researcher positionality, and a statement of it, is where the need to clearly delineate the oversharing of deeply personal descriptive narrative of self must reach a compromise with a theoretically driven analysis of potential to interpret, understand and articulate. To fail to do this as an "insider" undertaking research is to diminish the process of interpretive praxis and to invalidate a claim to authentic knowledge contribution from the context of applied professional practice.

Understanding self is a pivotal point in establishing positionality, truth and knowledge; and doing so shapes an acknowledged lens for reality through which lived experience can become a credible and authentic mechanism of making meaning of the subjective world within which we live and work. Fundamental to this is poststructuralism, which ensures the capacity of critical introspection to move beyond the systematisation of the inherently subjective, without losing capacity for trustworthiness and authenticity in self-examination and articulation of "being". Key authors such as Foucault and Derrida opened arenas of wisdom that provided contested stances against the need for existentialism, but which nevertheless enabled a critical orthodoxy of experience to have a poignancy it otherwise might not have gained in 20th-century philosophical circles.

The concept of performativity as elucidated by Lyotard also has a striking impact on individual capacity to express and articulate the meaning of experiential learning and positioning. What is of greatest significance to the deconstruction of long-held presuppositions and assumptions from individual realities and lived experiences is his acknowledgement of the fact that structuralist approaches denigrate and largely ignore the intraneous and extraneous figural components, which serve to function beyond the constraints of representational frameworks and structures. Positionally, Lyotard states the mutual reciprocity of the two and the relative implications of this to fundamental fields of academic disciplinarity such as linguistics and phenomenology. Perhaps most significant to research praxis was Lyotard's acknowledgement of the relevance of temporal and spatial specificity, which links directly to the situated nature of research-based practice. Experience and experiential articulation of sensorial self in an external world, therefore, become imperative to the credibility of language structure and discursive accounts of it. This essentially destabilises traditional thinking, ensuring that the world of interpretivist research remains free to celebrate the value of ambiguity and chaos that is a life lived and to abandon all hope of binary thinking in consideration of a "real world". It is this stance that permits us to frame professional identity in the context of truth, positionality and knowledge as epistemic reflexivity, in contrast to purely descriptive autobiographical narrative. This is in keeping too with the dynamic shifts in professional identity that a career trajectory based in the midst of politics, governmental change and upheaval, and consequently professional practice, can ensure.

Ultimately, what is researched will be dependent upon an individual driven need to know more of a particular circumstance. What provides legitimacy and credibility is the capacity to make transparent an epistemic positional stance and the relativist nature of this to epistemic reflexivity and, perhaps most importantly, how this is pragmatically reported in terms of ease of accessibility.

In the context of epistemic reflexivity, it is possible to regard the inter-relationship between knowledge and truth through a lens of reality that can dispel power relationships and discourses and facilitate the reconstruction of perceived realities in practice. For professional doctorate students, in particular, this ensures that emphasis is placed far beyond disciplinarity, so that upon successful completion of their learning, students have a sense of epistemic change and development that extends beyond the professional to the personal. This is a move away from the notion of Aristotelian mastery towards an authentic capacity for grappling with the complexity and ambiguity that frames research in the real world.

Personality versus positionality: Squaring the circle of power dynamics

Undertaking research in the context and setting of the workplace, which many professional doctorate students do, necessitates the positionality of the researcher being recognised in terms of their own instrumentality in the process. It is the inherent personality of the researcher that determines their adopted stance on such issues as politics, faith, cultural perspectives on gender, class and education, which are a consequence of their life experiences to date. All these are essentially epistemic variables that can ultimately impact on the researcher's capacity to interpret qualitative data and to recognise and articulate emergent meaning. To provide a degree of transparency to this was something relatively new to philosophy through to the latter part of the 20th century, but it is something that has obtained seminal resonance in the articulation of insider perspectives in critically reflexive research.

The importance of context and situation to the concepts of trustworthiness and authenticity are imperative considerations. These variables, as well as being a basis for value judgement on behalf of the researcher, can also marginalise and impact on the power bases inherent in the data collection processes, hence providing a capacity for marginalising and delineating life worlds that the researcher has been aiming to capture.

Providing an insight into researcher positional stance does not detract or ameliorate the concept of bias; it simply provides a transparent lens through which it can be acknowledged in the research process. The process of interpretation is dependent, then, on the interrelationship between the interpretive capacities of the researcher in making meaning of what the research participants report having made meaning of themselves. The complexity of this is self-evident, from the potential for losing the actual meaning-making in the processes of abstract thinking and interpretation, and from the perspectives of both the research participants and the researcher (Eisner, 1998). Eisner provides an insight into how this instrumental utilitarian approach allows a degree of believability, since it is presented with a degree of coherence and relative systematisation that enables the capture of themes in practice. This nexus between the nominative and the accusative in pragmatic terms enables the authentic recognition of the dynamism of social positionality and the temporal significance that rests within it (Eisner, 1998).

Self-reflection and positionality

Capacity for critical introspection, reflection and reflexivity are the skills necessary for the establishment of researcher positionality. It is important to frame where positionality actually lies on two fronts, namely:

1) Personal positional stance
2) Positional stance of the research inquiry

New researchers often do not differentiate between the two, but these are important since personal perspectives may not always align with the approach to the research. In this sense, it is important to return to the concept of question-led research, where the question to be answered is then framed in appropriately aligned ontological, epistemological and methodological approaches which, as a consequence, can then be conducted via appropriate methods.

The notion of being an insider or an outsider in the research process hinges on these considerations. Empirical research methods such as randomised controlled trials necessitate complete objectivity, since they seek to eliminate all bias and strip things down into intraneous and extraneous variables, which can ultimately be controlled or manipulated in order to attribute effect. However, interpretivist research involving the capturing of lived experiences and perceptions calls for an approach that can acknowledge the researcher as an integral part of the lived experience, where their impact on the data collected can also be acknowledged, sometimes as an integral part of the co-construction of knowledge in practice.

Epistemologically speaking, there is no right or wrong/better or worse approach to research inquiry and investigation; rather, equal but different approaches to the ascertainment of new knowledge from differing ontological and epistemological perspectives prevail as the best approaches to adopt. However, what ought to be acknowledged in the context of new knowledge development is that, since much research occurs in the workplace, the data collected in relation to professional practice will ultimately be impacted upon by the situated nature of knowledge, culture and context. To imply otherwise would be naïve at best and untrustworthy at worst. What this chapter aims to do is to facilitate researchers in understanding how to challenge long-held presuppositions and assumptions that are rooted in their personal and professional experiences, so that they can begin to think systematically, theoretically and in an integrated manner about the establishment of new knowledge in practice.

Certain elements of researcher positionality are fixed simply by virtue of who we are: our race and gender being the most obvious examples. It is these aspects of us that can only be acknowledged, not adapted or changed to fit particular fields of research. So, for example, a male undertaking research on the experience of menstruation has no experience of this physiological occurrence, whereas a female undertaking the same research might have. In terms of referential positionality, the two researchers as interpreters might have differing lenses of interpretation that are influenced by their gender. What matters, actually, is the acknowledgement of this in practice, so that readers of research can grasp the lens of interpretation through which both work. While these fixed aspects of who we are are important, they do not necessarily frame our positionality, hence the need to articulate them in research-based practice.

Returning to the themes of critical introspection, reflection and reflexivity, it is possible to break down interpretation into how affective domain beliefs, such as value judgements and personally held beliefs and assumptions, can influence the consequent construction of meaning of the world around us. Being able to locate a sense of self is pivotal to the capacity of authentic researchers in being able to ascertain how they might potentially influence the research process.

Paradigmatic sufficiency or the need to examine teleologically where research sits on that wider continuum is important in any discussion of researcher positionality and the positioning of research inquiry. Eliminating the perceived gap between interpretivism and empiricism is essential here, since all research and research approaches sit on one continuum, and positioning within it ought to be determined by the research aim or question most appropriate to answer, rather than a personal preference for a particular approach.

Our mechanisms of interpreting reality are articulated both by the written and spoken word, and as such there can be no conception or claim of objective reality in relation to any of the research we undertake. However, empirical studies, in particular, allude to this. Within the context of human endeavour it ought to be remembered that linguistics is a discipline rooted in social construction. Therefore, as the world is experienced individually so are also the meanings ascribed to it, and the choice of linguistic phraseology used to describe it is as individual as the experiences themselves. Establishing researcher positionality therefore necessitates a high degree of critical introspection on the personally held philosophies, political allegiances and theoretical perspectives that we align ourselves with, and on how they might potentially influence the way that we articulate findings to questions that we may be specifically motivated to ask in the first place. This, though, can also be criticised: if self-awareness is lacking, then positing the "self" within it may also be fundamentally misaligned or fundamentally wrong.

It is here that the notion of verisimilitude or the assumption that something is true rather than actually being confirmed as absolute truth ought to be considered. The fact that positionality in itself is socially constructed is a contentious issue in relation to epistemological approaches to the establishment of truth. Perceived and actual reality are very different, and it is this acknowledgement that consolidates the prospect of optimising levels of trustworthiness and authenticity in research-based practice.

Pragmatism as a concept has an obvious role in the context of establishing truth in research-based practice. What is so positive about pragmatism from an epistemological perspective is that it enables researchers to avoid the burden of heavy purist philosophy in their intellectual and vocational endeavour (Savin-Baden and Major, 2013: 21–22). However, this also ought to be counterbalanced by the need for researcher positionality to be established from a position of human interpretation, which is adequately framed in the need to be purposeful or useful in a practical context.

Intuition

As the whole emphasis of workplace research is placed on the sensorial awareness of experience from professional practice, the notion of intuition and the role intuition plays in the motivation and formulation of new knowledge cannot be ignored. Whether belief based on intuition is knowledge is a long-contested debate, and perceptual reality occupies the same philosophical reasoning space. Since perceptual realities also lead to belief via sensorial experience, then to frame intellectual understanding in this seems reasonable, which in turn makes it constitute knowledge, regardless of whether or not it is true. The notion of making sense of intellectual awareness can be regarded as socially constructed knowledge formulation, regardless of how abstract the intellectual awareness actually is. For either to be possible it is necessary to first distinguish intuitive from perceptual knowledge. Perception is inherently more advanced than simply having a sensorial experience or an acknowledgement of externality. The two are inextricably intertwined in the sense that perceptual reality is largely dependent upon *a priori* knowledge of sensorial experiences.

In the context of the social world, there is no singular truth but a continuum of truth which acts as a lens of interpretation for the execution of pragmatic research. This stance is termed relativism. Relativism is often closely associated with the concept of triangulation, in particular the triangulation of research findings from the context of research-based practice or practice-based research or, most often, work-based research. Triangulation might be used to assess congruency or consistency rather than repeatability. The concept of the testifiability of knowledge is largely redundant because of the temporality of knowledge, i.e., it is only true for that particular snapshot of time within which it is captured. Multiple realities within the context of positionality are also worth considering, since human perception is subject to maturation, change and adaptation in the light of additional human experience and perception. This in itself raises important debates in relation also to what perceptual knowledge is.

Delineating what is perceptual and what is sensorial is a key mechanism of distinguishing between different states of mind and the meaning the mind makes of information supplied to it. The fact is that being sensorially aware of something is inherently different from perceiving it. The two are very much interrelated in that it is possible to perceive without first having had sensorial experience of something. There is a non-stasis of positionality that aligns with this, which accounts for this capacity for change. For each perception in the world, there is a representation of a propositional truth about the world. In this sense, knowledge that derives from human perception is therefore experientially valid, but not necessarily true. This forms the basis of the distinction between perceived and actual reality.

In the context of the professional doctorate, where decision-making is fundamental to all stages of academic study from research design through to eventual execution and dissemination, the seminal work of Tversky and Kahneman (1974) from the discipline of economic psychology is most overlooked. "Judgment under uncertainty: Heuristics and biases" remains as relevant to the context of human decision-making today as it was at the time it was published, when it challenged the theory of human rationality. It is the situated context of workplace ambiguity that lends itself so well to the concept that uncertainty impacts upon the human capacity to make informed decisions. What Tversky and Kahneman revealed was the predictability in those errors of judgement made in the context of ambiguous evidence and in the face of multi-combinatorially framed complexity, where several intraneous and extraneous variables might be at play. They framed the terms heuristics and biases as explanatory mechanisms of the subconscious mental shortcuts that underlie automatic decision-making in applied praxis. The methodology that examined the interpretive and analytical ways surrounding their approaches to heuristics modelled exactly how high-level quality interpretation is fundamental to correspondingly high-level criticality in academic writing and professional practice. Those subconscious processes underpinning this are pivotal to the function of the human mind, and have provided a platform of psychological theory and conceptual thinking that has not only shaped modern-day economics, but has transcended disciplinarity to relevance to every academic and applied discipline where subconscious thought can sway and influence sense-making of ambiguity in practice. With a background in military psychology, Kahneman had been responsible for the assessment of soldier capability; the fact that he had been raised in a war-torn country provided the emphasis he needed to have an intellectual preference for applied rather than purely theoretical knowledge, and the influence that this could have on capacity for valid decision-making. Recognising the subconscious influences impacting on human judgement was a landmark in the study of human psychology, and one which later earned Kahneman a Nobel Prize. Tversky died before the same honour could be bestowed upon him for this collaborative work, which changed the face of economic behavioural psychology in the 1970s.

Decision-making in practice

The erroneous decisions that stem from applying automatic judgements in the process of complex decision-making were identified by Tversky and Kahneman (1974) as attributable to two concepts. These were termed heuristics and bias – the two are subtly but significantly different in terms of their impact on practice. Cognitive bias constitutes systematic errors in thinking, which can often be attributed to the nature and presentation of problems. This challenged the model of rational choice theory that had fundamentally underpinned social scientific research at the time. The authors highlighted the limitations of human cognition and how the reality of human decision-making is rooted in the capacity of humans to know the outcome of options available to them. Fundamentally, and of exceptional significance to practice-based learning and research, Tversky and Kahneman provided a means of educating members of society in being able to understand that the limitation of human reasoning is shaped by the subconscious biases that frame human thinking. Important considerations of human emotion in the context of departing from rational thinking were considered in "Judgment under uncertainty". The resultant systematic errors in thinking when people are emotionally impacted upon by issues are automatic, of which humans have no subconscious control. As such, the complexity of human nature is one which has to be considered in any aspect of research claiming to be purist in its objectivity, since it is debatable whether this is achievable at all.

Social scientists had traditionally posited decision-making as being either descriptive or normative – the delineating features of which are that description posits experience in the past, whereas a normative approach advocates reflexivity. Placing cognitive limitation at the heart of what it is to be a human making decisions opens avenues of understanding that had never been recognised before, and which are of huge relevance to professional doctorate researchers today as they are challenged in identifying workplace issues for address, understanding and wider dissemination. Ambiguity adds another dimension to reasoning capability, and what Tversky and Kahneman highlight before all else is that the unlimited cognitive capacity to predict certain outcomes simply does not exist in the human brain, since cognitive capacity for it is limited. While the majority of professional doctorate students will not need to formulate mathematical models for the comparison of human judgement with mathematical benchmarking tools, Kahneman's capacity to do this illustrated the assertion that clinical decisions made in the context of professional practice by humans are more error prone than those decided upon algorithmically by machines, which has shaped western societies in their bid for progression in the field of human judgement.

Defining the study of heuristics is relatively straightforward when applied to human decision-making. Heuristics are the cognitive illusions that minds use to bypass complex decision-making and, as a consequence, they are often unintentionally wrong. In the same manner in which heuristics are context specific and bound by the situated nature of key events and practices, so too is validity, which has important ramifications for the concepts of perceived and actual reality, verisimilitude and trustworthiness in practice. It is the predictability of heuristics and the consequent errors that manifest from them that are tangible and, in this respect, predictable. Within "Judgment under uncertainty", the three heuristics identified for specific concern are the concepts of representativeness, availability and adjustment (otherwise termed anchoring). Stereotypical assumptions fall under the bracket of representativeness, where human judgement can be very evidently skewed by the precognition with which people enter the construction of meaning-making. Humans therefore construct perceptions of reality based on their previous experience and the presuppositions and assumptions they hold about them in practice. As an outcome of this, representativeness can be fundamentally wrong and, as a direct consequence, can ultimately lead to misdirected or simply wrong conclusions about the information available to us. The availability heuristic is dependent on how common an experience has been, the meaning attributed to it and the capacity of people to make meaning and judgement in the light of it. It could potentially account for the subtle nuances of organisational culture that go unnoticed because of their frequency. Memory is thus posited by Tversky and Kahneman to distort as well as inform judgement, leading to an increasing likelihood of human error. Their work at this point made significance of the connection between cognitive bias and heuristics. Whereas heuristics were benchmarks of context and time, cognitive biases are more straightforward systematic errors of thinking.

The acknowledgement of heuristics

Kahneman was later keen to clarify that this connection does not necessarily denigrate heuristics as something bad, but rather something to be acknowledged and aware of. What it did, though, was frame intuition as something fundamentally flawed, but nevertheless valued in the absence of wider knowledge access at given points in time (Kahneman, Slovic, Slovic and Tversky, 1982). The wider implication of this historical research is that it identified a dualistic model of thinking, in which at some of the time we think quickly, intuitively and rashly, which is prone to error; and in the other part of the time we are considered, reflective and less influenced by the mental shortcuts that characterise quick thinking. It is these which have consequently been used to explicate human capacity for reasoning and the projection of behaviour in practice. Schwartz (2000) developed and extended this work on human emotion in practice and attributed it to the fuelling of heuristics in the formulation of subjective opinion. The notion of conscious brain activity is central to the context of critical thinking, critical introspection and reflexivity. Claxton (2015) highlights how so many aspects of human experience lie in stark contrast to the concept of common sense that we would like to think characterises personhood, as somehow making us credible as a species. While intellectuals may disagree on the subtle nuances of what constitutes the conscious awareness of the human mind, it is startling how their consensus collides in the context of humanity being inveterate storytellers, who automatically make meaning of the world around them, then assimilate it into a story to be told. It is a distinctive characteristic of the species that delineates and disarticulates it from the rest of the animal species occupying the world. It has sustained humankind for generations in our capacity to provide explanation and rationale for being and perceiving. Experience belies all perceptual reality and the mind, in all its complexity, is responsible for the glory of what is now badged under the label of human experience. This capacity to formulate and regale stories, whether to ourselves or to others, is pivotal to the process of being able to reflect and consolidate knowledge of what has been, what is and what has the potential to be in the world.

Collective narrative provides a context for the establishment of sociocultural context and history, and works far beyond the context of description and elaboration, by being able to frame future action and dependency on pre-existing meaning. Storytelling is intergenerational, cross-generational and characterises us as distinct in being able to traverse and incorporate representations in a process of sense-making that characterises existence itself. Claxton's (2015) observation that the perceptual world exists on the outside and that memories, thoughts and feelings are on the inside does much to unpack the significance of the unconscious mind in action.

The temporal nature of consciousness is also something of huge significance to experience, particularly experience of a particular point or time in history. Key words amidst our capacity to make sense of things are rationality, sense-making and explication. How fantastic it is, then, that the most celebrated of human achievements are characterised by the capacity to take risk, think laterally and thrive on ambiguity and the complexity of human life on earth. This does not deliberately or flippantly question our capacity as unique creatures, but addresses the beautiful irony that frames our existence and the meaning we ascribe to it.

The structure and agency of experiential being

Structure and agency have determined that the situated nature of experience is specific to our life trajectories, individual experiences and personal perceptions of them. For every context-specific interpretation, there will be as many realities of it as there are experiencers of it. It is here that the fundamental question of how we can prioritise and give salience to emergent themes becomes an issue. Locating the specifics of our own situated nature as interpretive researchers, making experiences of these realities, is imperative to this process of acknowledgement. Failing in this respect lends itself to the processes of overgeneralising and making universal claims about the value of data interpretation, rather than making specific, informed decisions as to whether emergent theory may have potential transferability to similar contexts and settings. Constraints of the process lie in the capacity of researchers to be sufficiently reflective and reflexive in accounts of themselves. The process is inherently reliant on self-evaluation and the acknowledgement and meaning of self that not all interpretivist researchers necessarily achieve. Perhaps it is the difficulty of recognising and critiquing concepts of personality, as opposed to just positionality, which makes this discourse so potentially challenging in practice. The concept of the personal, as opposed to the purely positional, integrates the concept of emotional intelligence into the dilemma of how best to present self. Personality itself can be seen as a paradigm influencing interpretive stance. Simplistically posited, the unique universality of human experience from the perspective of all individuals means that interpretivist approaches to research, arguably like any other human research, are influenced by the combinatorial variables that shape and inform the human mind. Personality can be defined, though, as the paradigmatic characteristics of perception, thought, feeling and behaviour expression that can differentiate one individual from another, and which are recognisable between temporal and situational contexts. Emotional intelligence hinges on all of these and, for the majority of people, personality remains fundamentally stable throughout life. It is this which can influence chosen ontological and epistemological stances as opposed to the specific ontological or epistemological stance of the questions and research areas we propose for study. However, as we are unique individuals, these are also all inherently unique. The implication is that our personalities can be argued to be the sum of our positionalities, although this can be contested with debates of whether personality is socially constructed. It is not our aim through this text to debate this sociological frame of perspective, but it ought to be recognised that, for the large part, the concept of human universality actually transcends situation, context and time, and that this is what actually frames human research endeavour.

Critical introspection, then, becomes a tool for analytically framing positionality and how elements of the self can ultimately impact on the execution of research. Specific academic disciplines can provide a means of prestructuring understanding, which is ultimately characterised by specific epistemologies. Where the disconnect of these epistemologies at a disciplinary level takes place shows that, from the earliest stages of research education, we have essentially limited the capacity of researchers to effectively and constructively align the ontological and epistemological bases of research with what could feasibly become their methodologies. Alvesson and Sköldberg (2009) assert that capacity for critical introspection is limited, because the domination of seeing is hijacked by prestructured and formulated understandings of what we are able to see.

Conceptualising self has become an anchor for challenging long-held assumptions and presuppositions about professional practice. The notion of self-concept is contextualised and shaped by interrelationships with others; and ways of knowing are ultimately impacted upon by these complex dynamics. Social psychology and self-identification theories have both radically altered perceptions of power relations and organisational hierarchies, and our relative place in each. Being able to provide the basis for systematic inquiry into a specific aspect of professional practice, or organisational setting, often necessitates being able to effectively theorise and base research studies within propositional frameworks of inquiry that are motivated by epistemic processes of social identity that are, in turn, motivated by subjectivity and perceived reality. Organisational cultures and contexts are fuelled by the dynamics of collaboration, dissonance, capacity for group functionality and specific social groups; and the self-perception of individuals is pivotal to the success of these cultures and contexts. The capacity that individuals have to become categorised, classified and labelled is immense; but their position as organisational researchers provides an opportunity for them to extricate themselves from the practices in which they are entrenched, and to critically examine the transectional positions they occupy between the personal and the professional that ultimately frame these. The relative salience of this is evident in the context of their capacity to interpret and make meaning of the subjective basis of experience, and in their contribution to this in wider fora than simply their own story-making for storytelling.

References

Alvesson, M & Sköldberg, K (2009). *Reflexive Methodology: New Vistas for Qualitative Research* (2nd ed.). Thousand Oaks, CA: Sage.

Claxton, G (2015). *Intelligence in the Flesh: Why Your Mind Needs Your Body Much More Than It Thinks*. London: Yale University Press.

Descartes, R (1641). *Discourse on Method and the Meditations* (trans. FE Sutcliffe). New York: Penguin Books.

Eisner, EW (1998). *The Enlightened Eye: Qualitative Inquiry and the Enlightenment of Educational Practice*. Upper Saddle River, NJ: Prentice Hall.

Ellis, C (1991). Sociological introspection and emotional experience. *Symbolic Interaction, 14*(1), 23–50.

Gleiser, M (2014). *The Island of Knowledge: The Limits of Science and the Search for Meaning*. New York: Basic Books.

Hegel, GWF (1896). *Hegel's Philosophy of Right*. London: G Bell and Sons.

Kahneman, D, Slovic, SP, Slovic, P & Tversky, A (Eds) (1982). *Judgment Under Uncertainty: Heuristics and Biases*. Cambridge: Cambridge University Press.

Savin-Baden, M & Major, CH (2013). *Qualitative Research: The Essential Guide to Theory and Practice*. Abingdon, UK: Routledge.

Schwartz, N (2000). Emotion, cognition and decision making. *Cognition and Emotion, 14*(4), 433–430.

Tallant, J (2017). *Truth and the World: An Explanationist Theory*. Abingdon, UK: Routledge.

Tversky, A & Kahneman, D (1974). Judgment under uncertainty: Heuristics and biases. *Science, 185*(4157), 1124–1131.

5

THE HISTORY AND CONTEXT OF RESEARCH IN ART AND SCIENCE

John Fulton

Introduction

This chapter aims to explore the history of the relationship of art and science. It would, of course, take too long to give an account of all the artists and scientists throughout history, so the chapter will give an overview of the relationship between art and science. Starting with the early Renaissance, I will be examining the work of the Italian artist and mathematician Piero della Francesca, through which the synergistic approach to art and science is discussed, and then I will be looking at Dutch painting. Next is an examination of the advent of modernity and an exploration of how the controversy between Robert Boyle and Thomas Hobbes justified reasons for the seeming split and different approaches to knowledge production. The final sections are an examination of the return to the synergy in the later part of the 20th century and the early 21st century.

Piero della Francesca

The term "Renaissance man" is used to call what is, in today's terms, an all-rounder; that is, someone who is good at more than one thing. Leonardo da Vinci, for example, was involved and excelled in both painting and science and engineering. To illustrate this point further, I will explore the work of an Italian painter who was technically a precursor to many of the major painters of the Renaissance, but whose work captures this essence.

He is the Italian painter Piero della Francesca, who lived from around 1412 to 1492. He was born in the town of Borgo Santo Sepolcro in modern-day Tuscany to a successful merchant and the daughter of a nobleman. He is a renowned painter who has produced many masterpieces such as *The Baptism of Christ*. He also authored three books on mathematics: *Trattato d'abaco*, *Libellus de quinque corporibus regularibuos* and *De propectiva prigendi*. All three of these books were written in the traditional mathematical manner and are clearly original to della Francesca (Field 2005); they were written in a scholarly manner and explored general mathematical principles. In his last book, *De propectiva prigendi*, he discusses the geometry and geometric principles in his paintings.

The point is that della Francesca's paintings were based on geometric principles, the composition of his paintings were highly structured, and the figures were organised with detail and precision. Yet, at the same time, the paintings are considered to be great art and, as such, they have meaning at a number of levels: mathematically and geometrically they are precise, and they capture the essence of the scene and reflect much of contemporary history. A key example of this is his *The Flagellation of Christ*. Mathematically and geometrically, this painting follows very precise principles.

> It appears Piero used perspective in the picture for portraying his three-dimensional design with mathematical accuracy, and furthermore this design was fused with mathematical symbolism.
>
> *Wittkower and Carter (1953): 302*

Clark (1981) suggests that the black marble strip over the bearded man is the unit of measurement and the whole picture is based on this unit. Although this is not a view held by art historians, King (2007) argues that the painting is based on what is referred to as the "Golden Ratio".

> According to King, the epigram and the painting both hint at a ratio called the "divine proportion" or "golden ratio", which is aesthetically pleasing. It describes a line divided such that the ratio of the lengths of the two sections (A:B) is the same as the ratio between the whole line and the larger section (A+B:A).
>
> *Marchant (2007:490)*

As a painter he can also be celebrated. Aldous Huxley (1925), in his essay celebrating the work of della Francesca, discusses *The Flagellation of Christ* and describes it as such:

In the extraordinary *Flagellation* at Urbino, the nominal subject of the painting recedes into the background on the left-hand side of the panel, where it serves to balance the three mysterious figures of the foreground.

And Huxley goes on to state:

I am attracted to his character, by his intellectual power, by his capacity for making the grand noble gesture, and by his pride for what is splendid in humanity.

This interplay between scientific principles and art is perhaps best described by David King who, in discussing *The Flagellation*, puts forward a hypothesis which is summarised in an excellent article by Marchant (2007). As well as demonstrating the interplay of art and science, it also shows how the wider societal issues are reflected in the painting and how both the characters in the painting and the painting itself can have multiple meanings. It is also important to mention that King's ideas do not have universal acceptance and are disputed by many art historians (Marchant, 2007), but he does present a plausible account which illuminates the central argument of this chapter regarding, in particular, mathematical precision, great art and a reflection of the contemporary ideological and political concerns of the day.

King (2007) analyses *The Flagellation of Christ* in some detail and contextualises the painting, which is dated as being painted in the years 1455–1460. In 1453, the Ottoman Turks conquered the Byzantine Empire. King also highlights the historical figure Cardinal Bessarion (1403–1472), who converted from the Greek Orthodox position to Roman Catholicism and became a cardinal of that church. He was a highly influential figure of his time and was patron of the arts and science, though it is unlikely he commissioned this painting (Marchant, 2007). Yet, according to King, he is reflected in and is indeed central to this particular painting.

King came across an astrolabe, an instrument which was used by "astronomers in navigation and predicting movement of the heavens" (Marchant, 2007). The inscription on the back was:

Under the protection of the divine Bessarion, said to come from the work of the axis, I arise as the work of Johannes in Rome in 1462.

The astrolabe was thought to be gift from Bessarion to his protégé, Johannes Regiomontanus, a young instrument maker. The inscription was unusual both in wording and spacing and this puzzled King. King enlisted the help of one of his students, Berthold Holzschuh, who took a photocopy of the inscription, which he blew up to the size of *The Flagellation of Christ*. He put it against the painting and, in doing so, found names which linked to the painting and its figures. This explained the unusual composition of the inscription (King, 2007).

The figures in the painting and who is being represented are controversial and can, according to King, represent more than one person. To follow King's argument, the figures are identified by the inscription on the back of the astrolabe, and he puts forward that the man on the throne is Pontius Pilate, the victim being whipped is Christ and the turbaned figure is also Pontius Pilate, looking on. The turban gives the figure a Turkish look and this captures an important contemporary issue: that of the capture of Constantinople by the Turks, which happened in 1451. The three figures in the foreground and to the right are as follows: the man with the beard is thought to represent Bessarion; the young man in the middle is Regiomontanus; and five young men, all deceased former protégés of Bessarion, are thought to be represented by the last figure. This theory is not universally held by the art world; for instance, the art historian Kenneth Clark (1981) suggests that the figures represent the count of Urbino and his two advisors, Manfrello del Compi and Tommaso dell'Agnello, and that the painting was a celebration of the death of the wicked count.

Dutch art

While the composition of *The Flagellation of Christ* and its representation are controversial and not universally agreed, it is nonetheless indicative of the interplay of various elements and how what came to be disciplines in later times were integrated in the work of the painter. This is illustrated by a consideration of Dutch painters. Alpers (1983) gives in her book *The Art of Describing: Dutch Art in the Seventeenth Century* an account of the ways in which Dutch painting very much reflected the societal concerns of 16th- to 17th-century Netherlands. She illustrates how, at a time when the microscope and telescope were discovered, this preoccupation with the visual, by making objects larger and more accessible to the eye, was reflected in the paintings of the period. She argues that the scientific revolution had two strands, observation and experimentation, and it was observation that was reflected in Dutch painting. Alpers discusses how the camera obscura was used by Dutch painters to examine in detail an image or scene, and it was this preoccupation with perspective and views which characterised Dutch art and was indicative of the scientific concerns.

Alpers goes on to illustrate this by discussing the differences between Dutch and Italian art. Italian art attempted to tell a story or allow the viewer of the painting to "look in through a window", whereas the Dutch painter attempted to reproduce what the eyes could see. This is highly reflective of the scientific discourses of the time and the increasing importance of observation.

Boyle and Hobbes controversy

At around the same time in England, a controversy arose between Robert Boyle and the political philosopher Thomas Hobbes. Shapin and Schaffer in *Leviathan and the Air-Pump* (1986) discuss this in some detail, outlining both sides of the argument and, importantly, they relate the controversy to the wider societal concerns of the time. In doing so, they illustrate both how the controversy arose from the current political situation of the time and how a seemingly focused argument influenced wider societal issues and the separation of science and nature. While art was not discussed as such, nonetheless this debate represented the demarcation of science and art into two distinct camps and in a way which was articulated and accepted.

Robert Boyle developed an air pump based on an original design by Otto von Guericke, which consisted of a glass globe and a pump. The aim was to demonstrate the creation of a vacuum. As Shapin and Schaffer (1986) point out, the experiment operated on three levels: materially (that is, the creation of the pump); literally (that is, the ways in which the results were made known); and societally (how controversies were handled in the contemporary society). There was debate about how secure the pump was and, in addressing this, Boyle argued that the reliability of witnesses was very important, and the experiment must be both transparent and reproducible. As Collins (1987) points out when reviewing *Leviathan and the Air-Pump*, Boyle maintained that witness reliability came from the sole use of landowners and gentlemen, and not people pulled off the street.

The political philosopher Thomas Hobbes objected strongly to this approach to knowledge production. Hobbes in his book *Leviathan* laid down precise principles of knowledge production and argued that ontology and epistemology were intertwined in the production of knowledge, and that the production of knowledge involved rigorous and systematic argument and, as such, was the province of the philosopher. He stated that improper knowledge was priestly and scholastic knowledge was personal judgement and opinion (Shapin and Schaffer, 1986). In discussing the air pump, he maintained that alternative explanations could be offered for the results and, as such, the experiment was invalid. Shapin and Schaffer (1986) and Collins (1987) argue that the performance of the experiment was open to scepticism and what started off as art (that is, the art involved in the experiment) became "confused into science" until it became an "unthinking routine" (Collins, 1987).

This controversy between Boyle and Hobbes took place in the 1660s, at a time when science was advancing and there were inevitable controversies and debates. This period is also referred to as the Restoration of the Monarchy, when Charles II was restored to the throne following a civil war and the execution of the previous king, Charles I. There was a desire to avoid any conflict and the questioning of institutions such as the state and the established church, and the Clarendon Code set very clear parameters against which conflict could be determined. In dealing with controversies, Boyle created very clear boundaries or, as Shapin and Schaffer (1986) put it, a space in which debate could take place. In doing so, and in establishing reliable witnesses, he created what is now referred to as a community of practice (Lave and Wenger, 1991), which gives an organisation a structure.

Scientific inquiry was seen not in opposition to art, but as distinct from it. Hobbes argued that this was open and exclusive, that it was in the hands of a select few and was not the result of rigorous and logical argument. Hobbes saw Boyle's approach as an attack on society and, in creating this space for scientific endeavour, he separated science and the experimental method from society, and compartmentalised knowledge and knowledge production. Latour and Woolgar (1979) carried out an ethnographic study of a scientific laboratory and showed that results of experiments did not always provide clear and unambiguous evidence; scientists often have to make decisions based on scientific principles and the community of practice (Lave and Wenger, 1991), which is important in constructing knowledge

Latour (1993) considers the Boyle and Hobbes controversy as part of his wider consideration of modernity. Latour links Boyle with the natural world and Hobbes with the social world; he argues that Boyle attempts to reproduce the natural world in his laboratory, but it still exists independently. Similarly, Hobbes in his political writings suggested that humans make society, yet society exists independently of humans. Following this argument, the two worlds are interdependent and intertwined. Latour also discusses the concept of purification, which seems to be an attempt to separate and focus on two distinct entities and, in this case, to separate science and nature; whereas a hybrid is an integration of ideas (or science and nature) and considers things in an entwined and integrated manner.

The Boyle and Hobbes controversy was not directly about science and art, but rather about knowledge production; however, its repercussions did much to separate science and art. To use Latour's terms, purification of the scientific approach did much to separate sciences and, perhaps through its methods of inquiry, it became separate from other endeavours. This had implications for other disciplines. In many ways this was artificial, as Collins (1987: 823) states:

> Sociology of modern scientific knowledge first pointed to the skilful basis of experiment and the problem of replication, and showed how art is conjured into science time and time again until it becomes an unthinking routine. Shapin and Schaffer show how the trick was done for the very first time. They show how an experiment, a local, artful performance was first made to produce knowledge which was universally as applicable as philosophical reason.

Science is just as creative as art, although the trajectories are very different; a novel idea in science can, and usually does, take 20 years to come to fruition, whereas in art, ideas can be translated comparative quickly and enter the public domain in a much shorter period. As Latour and Woolgar (1979) state, knowledge is constructed in a community of practice and because of this, and despite the similarities, the purification has separated knowledge into compartments and, thus, a separation between science and art has come about. In the UK, the education system from secondary schooling onwards organises subjects tightly, and individuals are expected to make choices at a very young age. I can remember at 15 being asked by one of the teachers which side of the school I preferred: the arts (English, foreign languages, music and fine art) or the sciences (mathematics, physics and chemistry).

Late modernity and the postmodern era

Gibbons et al. (1994) suggested that there could be two approaches to knowledge creation and they labelled these as mode 1 and mode 2 knowledge. Mode 1 is unidisciplinary and was what Kuhn (1970) had discussed. Mode 1 knowledge is the knowledge contained in a specific discipline and, as such, is clear and focused; its production follows very clear and explicit methods of inquiry and develops a knowledge base. Gibbons et al. (1994) argued that many problems and issues in the workplace tend to be messy and involve a number of problems from outside the discipline. Mode 1 knowledge therefore often does not really address the problem and one needs to draw from a variety of disciplines to illuminate and address the issues. Mode 2 knowledge is transdisciplinary, applied in nature and addresses issues relevant to the workplace. This is similar to the hybrid as described by Latour (1993) which he maintains is part of modern life.

A synergy between disciplines is required and mode 2 knowledge does not recognise the two cultures (Snow, 1960); rather, it uses different disciplines to illuminate different aspects of a particular problem. Increasingly, people are seeing science and art not as two separate entities, but as disciplinary approaches which can offer different perspectives on various issues. An example of this is the ERA project, which is concerned with climate change and approaches the issue from four disciplinary perspectives: environmental sciences, philosophy and religion, social sciences and creative arts. The split between the humanities and sciences is discussed in CP Snow's (1960) essay entitled *The Two Cultures and the Scientific Revolution*, which advocates the drawing together of disciplines. As Snow (1960:4) states:

> I believe the whole intellectual life of western society has been split into two polar groups … between the two a gulf of mutual incomprehension sometimes (particularly among the young) hostility.

By looking at things through silos we are hindered and this can hold back progress and result in a lack of collective wisdom in society. Humanities can help with the dissemination of scientific information and make things accessible to people. Although Snow does not mention this, it is a return to the Renaissance and our friend Piero della Francesca. *The Flagellation of Christ* is, as we have seen, based on scientific principles; it also addresses religious and moral issues and expresses religious truths. It is a work of art that speaks to us on a variety of levels as well. This is something that can be seen at the Wellcome Collection, which "creates opportunities for people to think deeply about the connections between science, medicine" (https://wellcomecollection.org/what-we-do/about-wellcome-collection).

This point is illustrated in the case of AIDS and HIV. In the 1980s people were dying of a mysterious illness. It was discovered very quickly that the symptoms were caused by a virus which suppressed the immune system. The discovery of this virus involved epidemiological and medical knowledge and skills. Treatments were discovered and, again, these required skills from pharmacologists, medics and physiologists to produce the drugs; nurses, doctors and other health professionals were also involved. However, prevention was crucial and how to get the message across to other and very diverse groups was also very important. AIDS is not an illness specific to groups, but it first appeared and was associated with particular groups of people, and stigma and stereotyping needed to be challenged. Health promotion campaigns targeted both these groups and the general population, since many people assumed that as they were not a member of those groups, AIDS did not really affect them or had anything to do with them. A completely different knowledge set was required, and a different range of skills came into play which addressed these issues. Creativity, literature and art played a large part and many of the advertising campaigns were both thought-provoking and effective. They could engage with people and get the message across very power-fully. While not to compare the campaigns with great art, they did use a range of skills and spoke to people at a deeper level. An interesting project is the patchwork quilts on which people were asked to contribute a panel in memorandum; these quilts were then put on public display.

Early posters, particularly the "There is Now a Deadly Virus" public information campaign, came out at a time when the illness was very much in the conscious of people and attempted to get people to think about the wider issues in society. This poster, which used imagery to get powerful and important messages across, spoke to people at a deeper level and got them to think. This is not to equate advertising health promo-tion campaigns with the great art of the Renaissance, but they do contain images and communicate powerfully in a way that goes beyond words.

Pictures painted by the American artist Thomas Haukaas symbolise the Native Americans who died of the disease through horses without riders. These pictures formed part of a wider exhibition in Los Angeles' Tacoma Art Museum in 2015, which showed paintings addressing issues of AIDS and HIV. Art around AIDS was part of the awareness-raising campaign, but many used art to express experiences and the impact it could have on people's lives (Rhodes, 2015).

Discussion

Piero della Francesca approached his work through an integration of art and science in a holistic and individualised manner. This is clearly demonstrated by the characters in *The Flagellation of Christ*. There is much controversy about who the figures represented, but they are related to the wider community and are political people at a local and international level. For example, there are references to the taking of Constantinople by the Turks. In a consideration of art and science the political dimension continually arises, and there is not therefore a clear binary between the two, nor is there something intrinsically different between them which causes the division. Rather, trajectories are set by the political and circumstantial situation.

In 1962, Thomas Kuhn (1970) wrote in *The Structure of Scientific Revolutions* of the nature of knowledge and the organisation of knowledge into paradigms: each discipline has methods of inquiry, and a body of knowledge and any developments must be done in accordance with this paradigm. Only knowledge which is produced in accordance with the paradigmatic approach is valued. All goes well until principles are questioned and/or a discovery is made, which takes things in quite a different direction; this is referred to as a scientific revolution. After that revolution, things settle down and the status quo is re-established. To return to Boyle and Hobbes, Boyle set out the paradigm for scientific inquiry, following a controversy or revolution. Of course, this is not revolution in the sense of the French Revolution, which involved violent overthrow of a particular regime. Boyle and Hobbes lived through the overthrow of the monarchy, the establishment of the Commonwealth and the re-establishment of the monarchy. Their controversy and debate were tame in comparison, and were certainly non-violent, but nevertheless were important and established a set of rules and managed a clear and distinct separation.

While Shapin and Schaffer (1986) and Collins (1987) did not explicitly draw on Foucault, the concept of discourses does much to explain the development of science and the compartmentalisation of knowledge. Foucault maintained that history is full of disjunction which can produce ideas that then take things in very different directions. The English civil war was one such disjunction; it left a reluctance to engage in any great controversies, and thus the space Boyle created for dealing with a controversy within a specific community came into existence. This allowed for discursive practice and subsequent knowledge production, which became increasingly specialised. Snow's (1960) essay considers that the split was a response to the increasing value being placed on science by society, and he laments that the humanities are separate from the sciences. He argues that the sciences need the humanities and that such a separation is detrimental for the development of the country. He is writing from the point of view of a scientist and can see the value of the humanities in communicating scientific findings and in general engagement with scientific endeavours.

The knowledge production and discursive practices continued. The idea of a community of practice (Lave and Wenger, 1991), where knowledge is produced within a framework of a discipline or out of practice, is important. The communities of practice reflect and reproduce discourses. Thus, the experimental method of Boyle has been considerably developed in science, although, as we have seen, decisions are made within a particular disciplinary framework. Arguably, perhaps the purest form of the experiment is medicine, with the randomised controlled trial and strict experimental protocols and procedures. This has given rise to the discourse of evidenced-based medicine. This discourse is particularly strong and rigidly controls knowledge production. This is to suggest that it is a negative or bad thing and is for the good of humanity. Interestingly, while not combining art and science, the patient experience is being increasingly recognised, and randomised controlled trials often have a qualitative dimension which examines context and experience. Patient narratives and their stories are being recognised and, while much is in a written format, auto-ethnographical accounts express themselves in variety of media.

In the later part of the 20th century, a transdiplomacy approach had been advocated (Gibbons et al., 1994) and art and artists are often included in this. This is not to relate art to mere explanation, but rather it is a way of adding to our understanding and conveying emotions in a very real and powerful way. The artwork based on the theme of AIDS and HIV is a good example of this, where, as well as conveying information, it is used to express experience and the emotions around the issue.

I have in the later part of this essay focused on the ways in which art can be used in science and, in exploring the issues, it seems very much a one-way street; one also gets this feeling when reading Snow (1960). It is art and the humanities that can be of use to science, yet other than developments in, say, paint, science is not of great use to art! However, one discipline which combines science (technology) and art is computers and technology; digital design is a well-recognised art form and many artists are using technology as a means of expression. Often, this requires knowledge both of art and of technology. One of the striking features of the Renaissance and Piero della Francesca is that it is the same person who is able to combine and significantly contribute to both science and art. In examining the 20th- and 21st-century developments and the generation of mode 2 knowledge, it is quite striking to see that it is different people who contribute the different knowledge components. So, despite the synergies, one cannot conclude that we have returned to the situation of the Renaissance. But art and science have a more positive relationship than Hobbes and Boyle; with the "two cultures" depicted by Snow, and with advances of technology and digital artists, we are beginning to see individuals who can contribute to both art and science.

Conclusion

There are many ways of dividing historical periods; the particular approach taken in this chapter is premodernity, modernity and postmodernity. Latour (1993) points out that this division is artificial and it certainly is when looking at knowledge and its development, which is much subtler. Nevertheless, the division is useful to consider the very broad approach to art and science taken in each of the epochs.

There is a separation of art and science, which is not to say that scientists cannot appreciate art and artists cannot appreciate or understand science and scientific discoveries. But the disciplines of science and art have very different trajectories and use very different methodological approaches. In premodernity, there was a clear interplay between art and science and there was not a division; both disciplines could be practised by the same people, as demonstrated in Piero della Francesca's work. This chapter aims to show that during the Renaissance this demarcation did not exist, and that artists like Leonardo da Vinci and Piero della Francesca drew on mathematical and scientific principles in their painting.

In the 17th century, the so-called scientific revolution brought about the division between art and science, or the purification (Latour, 1993). The division was artificial and had a questionable philosophical basis, but was highly influential and shaped things for centuries. In more recent times, there has been a return to an integrated approach and various disciplines have come to bear when examining particular issues or problems. It is not always in the same person, but various disciplines are recognised as being able to contribute and, while they may each have a distinct contribution, all do so in a unique way to address key and important issues.

References

Alpers, S (1983). *The Art of Describing: Dutch Art in the Seventeenth Century*. Chicago: University of Chicago Press.

Clark, K (1981). *Piero Della Francesca*. Ithaca, NY: Cornell University Press.

Collins, HM (1987). Pumps, rock and reality. *The Sociological Review*, *35*(4), 819–828.

Field, JV (2005). *Piero Della Francesca: A Mathematician's Art*. London: Yale University Press.

Gibbons, M, Limoges, C, Nowotny, H, Schwartzman, S, Scott, P & Trow, M (1994). *The New Production of Knowledge: The Dynamics of Science and Research in Contemporary Societies*. London: Sage.

Huxley, A (1925). Best picture. Available at: http://log24.com/log03/0813.htm

King, DA (2007). *Astrolabes and Angels, Epigrams and Enigmas: From Regiomontanus' Acrostic for Cardinal Bessarion to Piero della Francesca's "Flagellation of Christ"*. Stuttgart, Germany: Franz Steiner Verlag.

Kuhn, TS (1970). *The Structure of Scientific Revolutions* (Unabridged, 2nd ed.). Chicago: University of Chicago Press.

Latour, B (1993). *We Have Never Been Modern* (trans. C Porter). Cambridge, MA: Harvard University Press.

Latour, B & Woolgar, S (1979). *Laboratory Life: The Construction of Scientific Facts*. Beverly Hills, CA: Sage.

Lave, JW & Wenger, E (1991). *Situated Learning: Legitimate Peripheral Participation* . Cambridge: Cambridge University Press.

Marchant, J (2007). Science and art: A leap of faith. *Nature*, 446, 488–492.

Rhodes, M (2015). A sobering look at how AIDS changed Art in America. Available at: www.wired.com/2015/08/sobering-look-aids-changed-art-america/#slide-6

Shapin, S & Schaffer, S (1986). *Leviathan and the Air-Pump: Hobbes, Boyle, and the Experimental Life*. Princeton, NJ: Princeton University Press.

Snow, CP (1960). *The Two Cultures and the Scientific Revolution*. Cambridge, MA: Cambridge University Press.

Wittkower, R & Carter, BAR (1953). The perspective of Piero della Francesca's *Flagellation*. *Journal of the Warburg and Courtauld Institutes*, 16(3/4), 292–302.

6

PERSPECTIVES IN FAITH, ART AND SCIENCE

John Fulton and Andrew Livingstone

Introduction

This chapter will consider the relationship of science and religion and art and religion. The logical approach is to consider them separately: their histories are very different and the overlap and the debates are also quite different. The relationship of science and art is more complex and there are a variety of positions which can be taken, and much literature has been generated on these. Art in comparison seems less complex and perhaps more straightforward. This is not to suggest that there cannot be adversity of opinions and stances at an individual level, but as a discipline it is much more straightforward.

The section on science and religion will focus on the philosophical position and how, despite having seemingly similar ontological positions, this can lead to conflict or, at best, scientific and religious thought existing independently. However, there are some examples of an integrated approach and these will be highlighted in the chapter. While people can hold various positions towards religion (and science), art is not so polarised as religion and science, nor do people take such extreme positions on it. The focus in this chapter, and in keeping with the book's overall focus, will be on the transdisciplinary nature of work and its reflection on art and science.

It is thus hoped to give an overview of the current positions in what is a complex field and indicate the areas which are worthy of further investigation.

Science and religion

The relationship between religion and science has a long and complex history. In this chapter we will give an overview of the key issues and, in doing so, the focus will be on the Christian religion. There is an acknowledgement that relationships between other religions is both interesting and a fruitful area which could be explored, but because of limited space, the focus will be an overview through the Christian perspective. Similarly, the term science is used in a general sense, but with recognition that science is made up of a number of disciplines and often very different issues.

History

The first important point to make is that, as we use and understand them today, religion and science are fairly recent concepts. Before the age of Enlightenment and the 18th–19th centuries, science was looked at very differently. As for religion, it was conceptualised as a very different entity before the Reformation. Harrison (2015) discusses this in some detail and clearly articulates the argument that in the early days of Christianity, and up until the 16th century, religion was an inner disposition which later became an external codification. Pre-Reformation Christianity was not merely an external organisation; the Christian religion was an objectification of an internal reality and this is what Thomas Aquinas meant when he used the term *religio*.

Similarly, science was seen by Aquinas as an inner disposition or a discipline of the mind, whereas today we see science as an external body of knowledge. In the Middle Ages, scientific knowledge was a disciplined approach to thinking in much the same way as religion leading to a disciplined approach to behaviour. Aquinas maintained there are three virtues: understanding (*intellectus*), science (*scientia*) and wisdom (*sapientia*). These virtues came about through understanding.

> Science is a handmaiden not so much because it offers a positional theology but because it entails the performance of mental exercises that promote the personal transformation that is the goal of theology. Ultimate truths about divine things can be known only to the properly prepared mind; the study of nature was seen as contributing to the preparatory process.
>
> *Harrison (2015)*

It is also important to emphasise that the science of Aquinas was not science as we understand it today, but rather an understanding of nature and the natural world, and indeed this conceptualisation was evident right up through the late 17th and until the early 19th centuries. While Plato was concerned with the mathematical study of the heavens and Aristotle with the cosmos, Aquinas also saw theology as a concern with the external and immovable and natural philosophy as being movable. Nature was seen as a book which reflected God and thus was no different to scripture.

Post-Reformation, and perhaps because of the different religions which emerged, there came a period where religions were objectified and reified. This meant that dogmas and creeds were formulated and people had to ascribe to a particular belief system that was organised, rather than to an internal disposition, and there were also very clear alternative positions which could be taken.

Similarly, and a little later, science also became objectified and reified. Rather than, as Aquinas maintained, being a disposition or a way of disciplining the mind or a way of seeking God through nature, the sciences became established bodies of knowledge. The relationship between science and religion became more complex and they became two separate entities. There came about a split between science and religion and not only could they be viewed as different spheres of activity, but they also could be viewed as mutually exclusive. Rather than an integrated activity with the search for the divine as the common feature, there was a split which often was a chasm between the two areas.

Epistemological positions

There are ontological similarities between the two: both science and religion are realist; both believe that there are universal laws and universal truths; and it is the task of the scientist and theologian to uncover scientific inquiries and theological explorations, respectively. Although there are very different methodological approaches the central purpose is the same. Perhaps, because of this basic similarity, there have been clear tensions, and these have generated controversy and debate between the two with the relationship of science and religion having sparked much controversy. There are positions one can take and Polkinghorne (1998) presents a typology which illustrates the science and religion relationship and, in doing so, he outlines four positions which can be taken. They are conflict, independence, dialogue and integration of the disciplines.

Those who hold the conflict position see science and religion as incompatible and as actually being in conflict with each other. According to this position, one cannot, it would seem, hold both scientific and religious beliefs. A clear binary has been established. One of the chief advocates of the scientific position is the evolutionary biologist Richard Dawkins (2006), who maintains that belief in God is a delusion and who, in his famous quotation, sums up the position: "I am against religion because it teaches us to be satisfied with not understanding the world". On the religious side, the Galileo affair is often cited as an example of the antagonism between the two areas of activity. Galileo was deemed to be a heretic on the basis of his promoting of heliocentric theories, i.e., that the earth revolves around the sun. While the affair was complex and often oversimplified, it demonstrates the antagonism which can exist between the Church and scientific inquiry.

The independence position does not see science and religion as in opposition, but rather sees them as two mutually exclusive areas of investigation. Science is dependent on observation and empirical inquiry and the strength of its position depends on the quality of the empirical evidence. Religion does not depend on evidence as such, but rather on faith, and theological inquiry depends on scholarship based on logical arguments (Horsfield, 2017).

The third position promotes a dialogue between science and religion, rather than seeing the clear differences as a source of dispute or as activities which can exist in parallel. It is interested in promoting some discussion. The work of Harrison (2015) on the history of science is part of this movement. The genesis is said to have come from the work of Ian Barbour (1966). Barbour was an American theologian and in his book *Issues in Science and Religion*, he advocates a critical realist approach. Unlike the realist position, in which both endeavours are looking for an underlying truth which is contradictory (conflict position), or are seen as very different and independent areas of inquiry, critical realism holds the position that the goal of the scientist or theologian is to uncover the underlying reality. As humans we can only imperfectly understand reality, and this will change and develop as historical circumstances change and new discoveries come about that supersede the original position.

The work of the philosopher of science Thomas Kuhn illustrates this point. Kuhn (1970) said that rather than progress in a logical and linear fashion, the history of science was very much characterised by changes and disjunctions. There is within a discipline an approach in areas of investigation, with ideas that shape and direct the discipline and methods of inquiry which are recognised. To gain any credibility, workers in a field subscribe to the position held by their community of practice. This status quo becomes challenged and what Kuhn terms as scientific revolution takes place: ideas are reformulated and a new status quo is established. In other words, a scientific discovery challenges the existing status quo.

It can be argued in theology that the process is no different. In 1996 the Swiss theologian Hans Küng applied paradigm theory to theology, and he argued that theology was equally characterised by similar paradigms. Interestingly, Küng had previously lost his licence to teach as a Catholic theologian (The Holy See, 1979).

The fourth position is that of integration, in which science and religion are integrated. With the exception of the conflict position, none of the positions would suggest that scientists cannot have a religious faith, but the integrated approach sees science and religion as being integrated and that God is working in and through science. This approach is best described in the work of two men, both Jesuit priests and scientists: Georges Lemaître and Pierre Teilhard de Chardin.

Lemaître's theory was the primeval atom theory, which became known as the "Big Bang Theory". He did not see this as a way of expressing his religious faith or providing justification for the existence of God, but rather he saw theology and science as two independent activities. Whereas, in contrast, the French geologist and theologian Teilhard de Chardin saw the two as integrated; he was a strong evolutionist and he saw evolution as the argument for the existence of God. For him, in everything there is a fundamental unity and God is both the alpha and the omega, the beginning and the end. God is present in every minute particle and, for evolutionary theory, is the ultimate truth.

> Is evolution a theory, a system or a hypothesis? It is much more: It is a general condition to which all theories, all hypotheses, all systems must bow and which they must satisfy hence forward if they are to be thinkable and true. Evolution is a light illuminating all facts, a curve that all lines must follow.
>
> *Teilhard de Chardin (1980: 241)*

Interestingly, Teilhard's work was suppressed by the Church and he was not allowed to teach, whereas Lemaître's advice was sought by Popes Puis XII and Paul VI.

This typology is interesting, and areas of controversy are found in both conflict and integrated approaches, whereas science and religion and dialogue are much more palatable.

A poststructuralist perspective

So far, we have considered science and religion from both a realist and a critical realist position. One of the central ideas here is that language does not only reflect culture, but can also create it. Bruno Latour, a French sociologist and philosopher working in the postmodernist and poststructuralist domain, in his work examines the language and the positions which it can create. In his essay on religion and science, Latour (2001) explores and analyses the perspective of religion and science from a personal standpoint and from the insights gained through his ethnographic study into the scientific laboratory and the practice of science (Latour and Woolgar, 1986). His is very much a constructionist approach and he finds that, rather than following the strict scientific approach often depicted, the process of science is considerably messier and constructionist in its orientation, with data being revised and negotiated. There are several steps to be followed in any scientific project and any one of them could alter the project. From this standpoint, he compares science and religion.

Latour (2001) focuses on the modes of communicating within both areas of practice or, as he puts it, the regimes of enunciation. In religion, with a particular focus on Christianity, he argues that communication is performative, so that communication through the scriptures causes a change in behaviour and is therefore aimed to transform. The main point here is that is not done in a dramatic way, but in the ordinariness of everyday life. Religion for him is about the mundane and ordinary changes occurring in life, and to try and analyse them is to render them invalid. He turns commonplace assumptions on their head: religion and religious discussion are not about the transcendent, but are about the ordinary and mundane. Through the performative power of the language used in religions and scripture, it can, in the individual, bring about a transformation in their outlook and their approach to others.

Based on his insights into ethnography in the scientific laboratory, Latour maintains that rather than the objective rational activity that is often depicted, the scientific process is messier and much more interactive, with scientists discussing and interacting with others to create knowledge. The process of scientific development is long and involves a series of chains, and each one of the chains involves negotiations – some internally in the scientific laboratory, while others are with those outside, through the literature and thereby with the wider scientific community. The chains of events are long and can take different turnings and have very different outcomes. The process of science can lead to claims well outside of the laboratory. For example, the manufacture of a new drug finally ends up with it being given to patients to bring about a cure or to alleviate symptoms in some way. The practice of science can lead to grandiose assumptions and theory developments. Latour therefore argues that in contrast to our everyday beliefs, the practice of science is about the unseen and the transcendent, and can lead to wide-sweeping claims and, unlike religion, it gets us to take leaps and to look beyond the here and now.

Conclusion

There are a number of positions which people can take on the issue of science and religion. As such, this section represents the positionality of science and religion and does not offer an evaluative conclusion, but rather allows the reader to determine their own position in the debate(s). Perhaps one of the greatest interests is the integrated position, which highlights the ways in which a religion can be integral to the practice of science, although many devout Christians who are scientists can see the two activities as independent. Integration is both interesting and fruitful. While this section is Christian in its orientation, a consideration of other faiths is perhaps an area worth exploration.

Interestingly, Latour in his essay draws on examples from art to illustrate these points. I will highlight one of them. Latour points to a painting by Piero della Francesca, *The Annunciation*. Della Francesca was a mathematician as well as an artist and in his paintings, and particularly through his positioning of people, the perspective was mathematically very precise. In *The Annunciation*, the angel was painted as standing beside Mary rather than in front of her and is positioned beside a pillar. If the picture is blown up into three dimensions, the angel is not seen by Mary. Della Francesca was geometrically precise in his measurements; this would not be accidental or a mistake, but very deliberate. It illustrates the point that religious communication is focused on the everyday and is non-dramatic, but, as in the case of *The Annunciation*, it can have a profound transformative effect (Latour, 2001).

This example leads us to the next section where religion and art will be considered and the point emphasised that art can express concepts that are difficult to verbalise. Art as a medium can appeal to people at very different levels.

Art and religion

Over several decades, research within creative practice has explored the prefixes "inter", "multi" and "trans" with regard to disciplinarity, even negotiating and interrogating a "third space" – within contemporary art practice and critical theory. Boundaries have become blurred, have collapsed, are purely ignored or are interconnected in terms of a fluid approach to epistemological development and construction. This is significant with regard to research, particularly within creative/art practice that transcends existing boundaries and adopts a transdisciplinary approach.

It is useful first to bring clarity to the term transdisciplinarity. Marshall (2014) states that:

> Transdisciplinarity goes much further. It connotes a practice or domain that rises above disciplines and dissolves their boundaries to create a new social and cognitive space.

This so-called "new cognitive space" has gained ground within the academic landscape as researchers confidently create and explore new territories and ways of working that focus on the "research question", while simultaneously acknowledging and ignoring discipline boundaries. This approach can also be acknowledged with regard to art practice through both collaborative and individual application.

In reference to the context of this chapter, historically, religion was very much woven into the fabric of western society and with the Renaissance there came a rediscovery of the ancient Roman and Greek cultures. While the tradition of religious painting continued, artists such as Raphael drew from the themes of the classical world. The Reformation and the Counter-Reformation brought about a clear split in Christianity, yet religious art remained a major influence. It was with the Enlightenment and the development of science, as we know, and the associated increasing secularism in society that religious art was no longer a major force and that religion as reflected in art no longer maintained its dominant position.

There are numerous thorough academic and historiographical accounts of arts patronage (Paoletti and Radke, 2005; Strathern, 2017) and the changes that occurred post-Renaissance with regard to a separation of art and religion. This chapter does not set out to cover this well-researched and scholarly arena, but instead aims to focus on a contemporary contextualisation of transdisciplinary approaches to art and religion.

Contemporary positioning

Contemporary visual art and religion/spirituality exist in numerous formats that cover the spectrum from religious organisational commissioning (modern patronage), where the religious institution as patron still exists (albeit not on the scale of its historical highpoint), to atheist interpretation. The interface between art and religion/spirituality has a large remit and the connections and disconnections provide a wide canon for negotiation and interpretation.

The notion of the religious/spiritual modern patron is generally actualised through commission of an artefact, building or architectural feature (for example, a stained-glass window). The transdisciplinary nature of research and creative production will depend upon the rigid or flexible remit of the patron, and examples exist, from specific restoration or embellishment of historic buildings, to embedded religious iconography (found, for example, within the contemporary religious/spiritual buildings created by Tadao Ando), to the paintings of Mark Rothko created for spiritual spaces. Each of these will differ in respect of a transdisciplinary approach that can also be engendered by the infinitive nature of art and design research (Marshall, 2014). In this respect, innovative research, creation and implementation are enabled through transdisciplinary approaches that draw on the strengths of both spirituality and knowledge of sacred spaces and creative arts research and practice. To what extent patron control is negotiated will have implications for the creative process and approaches to research. As Barrett (2009) expounds:

> Because creative arts research is often motivated by emotion, personal and subjective concerns, it operates not only on the basis of explicit and exact knowledge, but also on that of tacit knowledge. An innovative dimension of this subjective approach to research lies in its capacity to bring into view particularities of lived experience that reflect alternative realities that are either marginalised or not yet recognised in established theory and practice.

This can prove difficult and contentious as epistemological understanding and gain will of course be rooted within discipline specifics for the production and interpretation of knowledge. In contrast, innovative research and new ways of thinking can be developed in the pursuit and production of knowledge through a transdisciplinary approach. As Morales (2017) states:

> If transdisciplinary work has the potential to generate innovative responses to the world's most pressing problems, it is paramount to identify the individual personality traits and skills necessary for reaching beyond a reductionist understanding of the world, to a complex view of interconnectedness.

Without a connectedness to religion/spirituality, a contested territory exists – an arena where artists are rejecting religion while maintaining aspects of spirituality (King, 2005). However, there is a developing interest in artwork emerging from a wider and diverse religious perspective (Morgan, 2002). Individual artistic interpretations and approaches to religion are often iconoclastic, ironic, subversive or even political. Categories for contemporary practice that incorporate the spiritual in art are constructed by Brown (1999), where he breaks down interpretation and negotiation of spirituality into the "exclusivistic", "assimilative", "alternative" and "pragmatic". These taxonomies are useful in navigating the contemporary relationships between religion/spirituality and art, particularly when developing a framework for research and when this moves beyond individual disciplinarity.

The contemporary art field in the last 30 years or so has witnessed several iconic "religious/spiritual" artworks; these include *Piss Christ* (Andres Serrano, 1987), *The Holy Virgin Mary* (Chris Ofili, 1996) and *La Nona Ora* (*The Ninth Hour*, Manrizio Cattelan, 1999). While there are a vast number of works, these stand out because of the media and political interest. Interpretation of religion through art ranges from the provocative to the lenitive and covers much ground in between. The works listed are iconic in the sense that they caused much controversy and were seen as blasphemous by some; hence two of the works were desecrated during exhibition. The artworks are representational in approach, depicting recognisable religious imagery and, as a consequence, the politicised and controversial element within the work becomes paramount. Less provocative or subversive approaches can be evidenced in *Untitled (Last Supper)* (Adi Nes, 1999) and, more recently, *Martyrs (Earth, Air, Fire, Water)* (Bill Viola, 2014). These works, although political in content, are visually less controversial; they offer critique (Green, 2011) and are imbued with qualities for negotiating the interconnectedness between art and religion within a contemporary context. Critique or "criticality" is fundamental to arts research, creativity and methodologies for exploration – with regard to transdisciplinary research, the questions, aims and methods should be developed in collaboration with all of those involved, including those who will be impacted by the work. This will be explored further through a project undertaken by the author.

Case study – a subversive approach

Ex-voto is an installation artwork consisting of ceramic objects, film and sound. The artwork forms part of a larger exhibition titled *Parallax View* commissioned by Tullie House Museum and Art Gallery. In terms of context, the "patron" in this instance is the museum – a contemporary version, one could argue, of the "Church as patron". However, a more fluid and expanded discourse is in place, one that engenders the researcher/artist, as commented upon by Dahn (2011), who states that Livingstone "occupied a range of positions: ceramist, installation artist, researcher, explorer, intimate, communicator, collaborator, writer…". This transdisciplinary or "collaborative" approach between museum, industry and artist simultaneously acknowledges multiple and singular positions and, in doing so, engenders epistemological gain, an observation supported by Morales (2017):

> The nature of art practice is to ask questions not yet asked, and find answers that have meaning and relevance based on our personal interpretations of the world. In the studio, researchers reveal multiple ways of knowing, co-develop knowledge, reveal relationships in context, and are motivated through individual passions and questioning.

It is interesting to observe within the quotation that art practice asks questions that are not yet asked; this appears to be one of the fundamental tenets of transdisciplinarity in that questions are not discipline-specific, but are co-constructed. While it can be argued that the museum/gallery falls within the field of art practice, research and application is very much a separate discipline. In this respect, the *Parallax View* project and exhibition of the same name began from a posed central research question based upon a historical collection of porcelain. The simple question "What would it look like now?" was explored by the museum/gallery, artist and industrial artisans, each with their own respective knowledge and expertise.

Ex-voto is a visualisation of the demise of the ceramics industry in the UK, an element of which is expressed through religious interpretation. For example, in the suspension of 1,200 bone-china limbs, a similarity is drawn with votive limbs hung in churches. Viewers sit below the suspended limbs to watch a film showing the creation of a ceramic figurine incorporating the various components carried out by factory workers/artisans during production. A sound art piece is overlaid within the gallery space that consists of a recording of bone–china limbs chiming; they are presented in the form of a religious chant and, more significantly, as a critical tool of expression (Rajguru, 2013). At the entrance to the installation space is a manufactured figurine, as evidenced in the film – the collective elements subversively offer a prayer to an industry in demise. As the artist within the project, I was central to the research; however, the project introduced and explored new lines of inquiry, developed alternative methodologies and, as a consequence, explored new areas within my own art practice.

The artwork engages religion through a subversive approach and implementation, utilising material, image and sound within a mimetic interpretation. In contrast to Serrano and Ofili's work, representational iconography is not utilised; instead, a subtle visual language is employed that engenders a critical political positioning.

Conclusion

The visual and theoretical landscape of art and religion covers a wide spectrum that demonstrates both connection and separation in terms of their relationship. Varied approaches and interpretations are in evidence, as both art and religion have numerous platforms and facets. In terms of research in this area, transdisciplinary approaches have helped to engender epistemological gain, a concern noted by Haseman (2009) over a decade ago:

> Practice-led researchers believe it is folly to seek to only "translate" the findings and understandings of practice into the numbers (quantitative) and words (qualitative), modes preferred by traditional research paradigms. They argue that a continued insistence that practice-led research be reported primarily in the traditional forms of research (words or numbers) can only result in the dilution and ultimately the impoverishment of the epistemological content embedded and embodied in practice.

This section has highlighted just a small area within the much wider remit of art and religion. Examination will naturally be directed by individual bias dependent on religious/spiritual belief and subjective art positioning. This conclusion does not aim to close down interpretation and thought for the reader, but offers possibilities in terms of engendering epistemology through transdisciplinary approaches to research.

References

Barbour, IG (1966). *Issues in Science and Religion.* Englewood Cliffs, NJ: Prentice-Hall, Inc.

Barrett, E (2009). Foucault's "What is an author?": Towards a critical discourse of practice as research (pp. 135–146). In E Barrett & B Bolt (Eds). *Practice as Research: Approaches to Creative Arts Enquiry.* London: IB Tauris.

Brown, GR (1999). Toward a topography of the spiritual in contemporary art. *New Art Examiner, 26*(6), 23–27.

Dahn, J (2011). A far cry from throwing a pot. In A Livingstone (Ed.). *Parallax View* (pp.62–67). Sunderland, UK: Art Editions North, University of Sunderland.

Dawkins, R (2006). *The God Delusion*. London: Black Swan.

Green, T (2011). Without a prayer: Does the art world hate religion? *Modern Painters, 23*(3), 28–30.

Harrison, P (2015). *The Territories of Science and Religion*. Chicago: University of Chicago Press.

Haseman, B (2009). Rupture and recognition: Identifying the performative research paradigm. In E Barrett & B Bolt (Eds). *Practice as Research: Approaches to Creative Arts Enquiry* (pp.147–158). London: IB Tauris.

The Holy See (1979). Sacred Congregation for the Doctrine of the Faith: Declaration. Available at: www.vatican.va/roman_curia/congregations/cfaith/documents/rc_con_cfaith_doc_19791215_christi-ecclesia_en.html

Horsfield, J (2017). *Fine-Tuned Faith: Science and Faith – Are They Compatible?* n.p.: Hearts and Minds Media Publications.

King, M (2005). Art and the postsecular. *Journal of Visual Art Practice, 4*(1), 3–17.

Kuhn, TS (1970). *The Structure of Scientific Revolutions* (Unabridged, 2nd ed.). Chicago: University of Chicago Press.

Latour, B (2001). "Thou shalt not take the Lord's name in vain": Being a sort of sermon on the hesitations of religious speech. *RES: Anthropology and Aesthetics, 39*(1), 215–234.

Latour, B & Woolgar, S (1986). *Laboratory Life: The Construction of Scientific Facts* (2nd ed.). Princeton, NJ: Princeton University Press.

Marshall, J (2014). Transdisciplinarity and art integration: Toward a new understanding of art-based learning across the curriculum. *National Art Education Association Studies in Art Education: A Journal of Issues and Research, 55*(2), 104–127.

Morales, MM (2017) Creating the transdisciplinary individual: Guiding principles rooted in studio pedagogy. *Journal of Interdisciplinary Studies in Education, 6*(1), 28–42.

Morgan, A (2002). Beyond post modernism: The spiritual in contemporary art. *Art Papers, 26*(1), 30–36.

Paoletti, JT & Radke, GM (2005). *Art, Power and Patronage in Renaissance Italy*. Upper Saddle River, NJ: Prentice Hall.

Polkinghorne, JC (1998). *Science and Theology*. London: SPCK/Fortress Press.

Rajguru, M (2013). Chanting in the gallery: Ritual sound and its phenomenology in contemporary art. *Journal of Visual Art Practice, 12*(2), 181–193.

Strathern, P (2017). *The Medici: Power, Money, and Ambition in the Italian Renaissance*. New York: Pegasus Books.

Teilhard de Chardin, P (1980). *The Phenomenon of Man*. London: William Collins Sons & Co.

CONCLUSION

Catherine Hayes

Knowing not just what we know, but also how we know it, is an integral part of understanding the core discipline of epistemology. We live in what is now termed a "knowledge society", driven by the temporal immediacy and availability of what can be known. We are hopeful that this book has provided an insight into the evolution of this process, from the Renaissance period through to the present day, and that it might be clear that the universal experience of knowing is influenced by political, human and social agendas; and that these are likely to serve as an ongoing basis for knowing.

Although separated by disciplinarities, taxonomies and academic parameters of praxis, what is clear is that in the unbreakable link between art and science, particularly, is the remaining commonality and connection between the construction and meaning-making of knowledge as perceived by humankind.

We hope that this short book may inspire you as a reader to look beyond the immediately apparent, to delineate between perceived and actual reality and to think twice before making a claim surrounding the nature of truth in your own practice. A major challenge in the contesting of epistemic assumption, or of positionality in research design and methodology, is how we best know ourselves, what we bring to a tabula rasa or blank slate and how best this can be acknowledged in the process of research. Being able to delineate between what is epistemic, metacognitive and cognate within all of these is imperative to the capacity we have to challenge our own thoughts and perceptions, which can ultimately influence how we interpret the world. We wish you every success as you undertake this journey, and hope that this short text will in some way help you think "outside of the box" as you do so.

Professor Catherine Hayes
June 2020

RECOMMENDATIONS FOR FURTHER READING

Catherine Hayes

The following short annotated bibliography of publications is of significance to our own approach in this text and we hope will further serve to develop readers' interest in the transcendence of disciplinarity in everyday research praxis. These are listed in alphabetical order and no particular degree of importance or precedence is placed on any recommendation.

Bernstein, JH (2015). Transdisciplinarity: A review of its origins, development, and current issues. *Journal of Research Practice*, 11(1), 1–20.

Bernstein's overview of the relevance of transdisciplinarity to both the contexts of research and education provides a fascinating insight into how crossing the boundaries of disciplinarity in practice ought not to be limited to traditional disciplinary paradigms. What is advocated is the construction of new knowledge via wholly new and innovative approaches to using the foundational basis of purist disciplinarity to shape the proposal of new principles and criteria for the furtherance of knowledge. What is particularly relevant is the consideration of the global world as an information society. We feel this work has particular resonance with our own contribution to the literature.

Bruhn, JG (1995). Beyond discipline: Creating a culture for interdisciplinary research. *Integrative Physiological and Behavioral Science,* 30(4), 331–341.

This paper recognises that, at the time it was written, interdisciplinary research was not a common research paradigm. The formative recognition that transcending disciplinarity necessitates progression beyond functional praxis to a consideration of the cultural and social perspectives of organisations has become the keystone of many work-based praxis doctoral degrees, such as the professional doctorate. This deviation from tradition at the time constituted contemporaneous thinking that now characterises much of educational and research approaches. As such, its relevance to current research cannot be underestimated and the paper itself provides an insight into both successful and unsuccessful ventures, which readers can reflect upon.

Eisner, EW (2017). *The Enlightened Eye: Qualitative Inquiry and the Enhancement of Educational Practice*. New York: Teachers College Press.
Eisner's legacy to discipline-based arts education was the development of the importance of forms of representation in both research and education. He seminally recognised that a dearth of the arts and the prominence of standards and standardised tests had resulted in a lack of appreciation for creative thinking in the classroom. His work not only paved the way for a greater recognition of creative practice as an academic discipline, but also framed the case for a deeper understanding of art to be presented in supporting the construction of new knowledge. This work typifies Eisner's passion for art to be extracted from the very public perception that art had a "monopoly over creativity". In relation to our own contribution to the literature, we believe that, as an integral part of our recommended reading, Eisner's work represents an invaluable contribution to knowledge.

Glanzberg, M (Ed.) (2018). *The Oxford Handbook of Truth*. New York: Oxford University Press.
While this is a more expensive acquisition than other texts on our recommended reading list, it is actually an invaluable resource in its capacity to link disciplinarity with the concepts of trustworthiness, authenticity and their relevance to knowledge and representation. As one of the finest compendiums of work available on the nature and relevance of truth, as well as its systematic representation in research arenas around the world, this will doubtlessly prove itself an invaluable and authoritative text for the discerning epistemologist.

Goldman, A and Whitcomb, D (Eds) (2011). *Social Epistemology: Essential Readings*. New York: Oxford University Press.
This is a "must read" for those engaging in the development of their understanding of systematic human inquiry. The variety of readings incorporated into the text ensures a broad, generalist overview of the theoretical and conceptual which, when applied in praxis, provide a firm basis for academic and researcher integrity. This is an accessible read, and a great preparatory text for all researchers seeking to frame social epistemology in the space between ontological and philosophical inquiry.

Solem, O (2003). Epistemology and logistics: A critical overview. *Systemic Practice and Action Research*, 16(6), 437–454.
Now a historical addition to the literature, this paper addresses issues that still remain current in a wider array of disciplines than logistics, which is where the work is specifically focused.

The paper provides a rigorous philosophical reflection on the methodological underpinnings of logistics, which can now legitimately be applied to other situations, contexts and academic and work-based disciplines. Logistics is used as a key exemplar of how traditional objectivist methodological suppositions and positivist theories of knowledge had been positionally dominant, but how new perspectives are providing an insight into the value of more interpretivist conceptions of social theory and subjectivist methodological suppositions. Perhaps the most salient point in this work is the recognition that neglecting to challenge the epistemology of a discipline may result in an entirely obsolete paradigm. This leads to the positing that by challenging underpinning metatheoretical assumptions surrounding any circumstance, and by actively reflecting upon them, a more holistic and multidisciplinary approach can be achieved.

INDEX